PERFORMANCE CONVERSATIONS

Thank you for your support!

Chris

Advanced Praise for *Performance Conversations* by Christopher D. Lee, Ph.D.

"Dr. Lee transforms the modern leader's approach to Performance Conversations with a potent framework for asking the questions that truly engage employees, improve performance, and ensure accountability."
—**Cy Wakeman,** *New York Times* bestselling author of *No Ego*

"A long-overdue game changer for anyone truly serious about performance improvement."
—**Dr. Ronald R. Sims,** Floyd Dewey Gottwald Senior Professor, Raymond A. Mason School of Business, William & Mary

"Dr. Lee reminds us in *Performance Conversations* that relationships matter, trust is critical, and there is a significant difference between a performance conversation and performance review. An excellent overview for the first-time manager and experienced manager alike."
—**Jeffrey S. Brody,** Chief Human Resources Officer, ManTech International Corporation

"*Performance Conversations* masterfully outlines the role and development of effective questions as a critical tool in any performance improvement scenario. This is a must-read book for any successful manager or leader in the 21st century."
—**Dr. Edward E. "Ted" Raspiller,** President, John Tyler Community College

"*Performance Conversations* is an extraordinary framework on the merits of why, how, and what engaged leaders do to build, form, and inspire teams to excellence."
—**Dr. James I. Van Zummeren,** Deputy Director, Lejeune Leadership Institute, Marine Corps University

"*Performance Conversations* offers practical insight and interactive tools to empower managers to have transformative conversations with employees—a must-read for all managers and organization leaders who are truly invested in their employees."
—**Mary E. Hagood,** Talent Management Consultant, Federal Reserve Bank of Richmond

"Wow, what can I say? This groundbreaking book by Dr. Lee finally replaces inflexible performance appraisal systems of the past with an easy-to-follow and effective *Performance Conversations* approach."
—**David G. Tomanio,** M.B.A, Ph.D., retired Assistant Vice President (CHRO) for Human Resources, Florida Atlantic University

"The best leaders help their team members see their own value and coach them to achieve their potential. Simple, but not always easy, *Performance Conversations* delivers a systematic, research-based, and reliable approach for building strong relationships, developing trust, instilling accountability, and achieving results together."
—**Scott Edwards,** Human Resource Manager, Anord Mardix

"Thriving employees are energized when empowered, properly guided, and supported through encouragement and active, ongoing coaching. In *Performance Conversations*, Dr. Lee shows managers how to develop this dynamic relationship to improve both engagement and effectiveness in organizations."
—**Amel Cuskovic,** Assistant Vice President for Human Resources (CHRO), Radford University

"Dr. Lee shows us there's a better way to engage employees and it all starts with having regular and meaningful *Performance Conversations*."
—**Bryan Garey,** Vice President for Human Resources, Virginia Tech

"Delivered in a conversational style and full of actionable concepts and communication templates, *Performance Conversations* will quickly find its place as a foundational resource for new and seasoned managers alike."
—**Jennifer K. Pittman,** M.S., SHRM-SCP, Associate Vice President of Human Resources (CHRO), Virginia Western Community College

"The swell of employees working from home has put the spotlight on performance management, so there's never been a better time to get it right. Chris gets it right, and with great clarity and detailed practicality."
—**Dimitri Boylan, Dimitri has a account Founder & CEO,** Avature

"*Performance Conversations* is a must-read for anyone who wants to improve employee job performance in a supportive and inspirational manner!"
—**Patrice Masterson, Assistant Director of Benefits, University of Georgia**

PERFORMANCE CONVERSATIONS

How to Use Questions to Coach Employees,
Improve Productivity, and Boost Confidence
(Without Appraisals!)

Christopher D. Lee, Ph.D., SHRM-SCP, SPHR

Society for Human Resource Management
Alexandria, Virginia I shrm.org

Society for Human Resource Management, India Office
Mumbai, India I shrmindia.org

Society for Human Resource Management, Middle East and Africa Office
Dubai, UAE I shrm.org/pages/mena.aspx

BETTER WORKPLACES
BETTER WORLD™

The Society for Human Resource Management is the world's largest HR professional society, representing 285,000 members in more than 165 countries. For nearly seven decades, the society has been the leading provider of resources serving the needs of HR professionals and advancing the practice of human resource management. SHRM has more than 575 affiliated chapters within the United States and subsidiary offices in China, India, and United Arab Emirates. Please visit us at www.shrm.org.

Performance Conversations® is a registered trademark.

Library of Congress Cataloging-in-Publication Data

Names: Lee, Christopher D., author.
Title: Performance conversations : how to use questions to coach employees, improve productivity, and boost confidence (without appraisals!) / Christopher D. Lee, PhD., SHRM-SCP, SPHR.
Identifiers: LCCN 2020023306 (print) | LCCN 2020023307 (ebook) | ISBN 9781586446697 (paperback) | ISBN 9781586446703 (pdf) | ISBN 9781586446710 (epub) | ISBN 9781586446727 (mobi)
Subjects: LCSH: Communication in personnel management. | Employees--Rating of. | Performance.
Classification: LCC HF5549.5.C6 L378 2020 (print) | LCC HF5549.5.C6 (ebook) | DDC 658.3/14--dc23

Printed in the United States of America

FIRST EDITION

PB Printing 10 9 8 7 6 5 4 3 2   61.15334

Contents

List of Figures and Tables

Figures

Tables

Foreword

All organizations care about performance. Whether you're for-profit or nonprofit, regardless of what's happening with the economy or the job market, all organizations care about performance because it's what helps organizations achieve their strategic goals. Frankly, employees care about performance, too, because they know their performance helps them to achieve their career goals. Great performance helps employees get the promotion they've been wanting, or the pay increase they feel they deserve.

Human Resources departments have traditionally used performance management systems to align organizational and employee needs. Contrary to some beliefs, HR did not dream up performance management systems as some form of punishment. But that being said, something different is needed for the modern workplace. Over the past decade we've seen a huge increase in technology, which has created changes in the ways we work. As a result, employees are more mobile and connected than ever before. That's a good thing, and it's also the reason organizations need to reexamine their performance management practices.

Everyone Is Responsible for Performance Improvement

I've had the pleasure of knowing Dr. Christopher D. Lee for many years. We first worked together as volunteer leaders for the Society for Human Resource Management (SHRM). So, I know from personal experience that he has firsthand expertise working in the trenches. This is important because Chris truly knows that successful performance management involves everyone in the organization.

This book makes it very clear that improvement involves conversations and those conversations need to happen at every level of the organization. *Performance Conversations: How to Use Questions to Coach Employees, Improve Productivity, and Boost Confidence (Without Appraisals!)* is the guide to making those conversations happen. Make no mistake, conversations are an art. Sometimes we think conversations (specifically performance conversations) are easy and anyone can do them with little or no training. Honestly, that's not always true, which is why this book is necessary reading.

Performance Improvement Is Focused on Answers

I was particularly drawn to a Zen adage in the book: "He, who forms the question, determines the answer." It reminded me that if I want to receive good information, I need to know how to ask a really good question because unfortunately, mediocre questions yield mediocre answers. If we really think about it, performance improvement is about unlocking the secrets (the "answers") to high performance. In this book, Chris shares with us how to formulate the really good questions necessary to unlocking those performance answers. I'm not going to give it away here, but Chapter 5 and the Magnificent Seven Questions should be required reading for every business professional.

That shouldn't be too difficult because while the book does dive deep into the questions and conversations that should happen between managers and employees, it also maintains an incredible flexibility. If your organization uses a very traditional performance management process, you'll find questions that can be incorporated into that style. They also work for organizations that have adopted a newer performance management model, like the ones with quarterly feedback sessions. Finally, I can see this book being used outside of the performance review process in coaching and mentoring relationships, which are equally focused on the importance of good questions and increasing productivity.

Organizations and Individuals Care about Performance

Performance conversations matter because organizations and their employees care about performance. However, only good performance conversations produce high performance. These conversations are exactly what employees, managers, and Human Resources departments need, and this book will provide all the answers.

—Sharlyn Lauby, SHRM-SCP
Publisher of the business blog HRBartender.com
Author of the bestselling book *The Recruiter's Handbook:
A Complete Guide for Sourcing, Selecting, and Engaging the Best Talent*

Acknowledgments

Thanks to the countless friends, colleagues, clients, and students who provided the ideas and inspirations which made this book possible. Jerry Armstrong, Liz Bare, Tracy Battle, Jay Cabana, Andrew Caleb, Connie Costigan, Bettye Ellison, Mary-Anne Gallagher, Melany Gallant, Mary E. Hagood, Marian Hassell, Susan Henderson, James Hickman, Brian E. Hill, Kelly Hockaday, Jennifer James, Mark Jankelson, Carla Kimbrough, Neil Morris, Jeff Nelson, Terri N. Payne, Catherine Puckett, Tashia Scott, Penny Sharples, Carl Sorensen, Victoria Waldron, David Ward, Dave Watkins and Melanie Young have all made me a better person, professional, and author. Acknowledgment and affection for the support of Amber Alexis Lee and all the Elgersman Lee ladies. Look, Mom, this is number four—if you are looking down here and counting.

Introduction

I know you won't believe me, but the highest form of
human excellence is to question oneself and others.

—Socrates

The Performance Conversations method is a performance improvement system. It has the singular goal of empowering individuals to reach their full potential at work. It is built upon a coaching model wherein a manager —the coach—provides the necessary guidance, support, direction, and encouragement so that the employee—the performer—is enabled to take ownership of their work and execute it flawlessly. It uses quality questions to involve the employee in thinking about their work and taking the right actions to increase performance. This approach stands in stark contrast to traditional performance appraisals that are negative experiences designed to rate performance, label employees, and document the past for a variety of confusing administrative purposes.

Coaches and Performers

The Performance Conversations method is designed to help employees learn to work better, perform better, and also feel better about their work. When employees are not at their optimum performance, they must learn to do things differently, develop new skills, and grow as people and professionals. In short, they must get better. The world's best athletes all have coaches, and no one goes to the Olympics without a coach and expects to win. Why would employees go to work and expect to achieve *A+* outcomes without a great coach—their manager? Great performances are actually great co-performances—they are the byproducts of a great performer and coach duo.

In addition to the training, guidance, and insight a trusted coach provides, employees perform better with help. Some days are better than others, and sometimes we fall short of our goals. Other times we have self-doubt, develop bad habits, or lose our way—it happens to the best of us. These are the times when a comforting word, a kick in the butt, a challenge to get back into the fray, or simply having a cheerleader on the sideline really makes a difference. After triumphant gold medal athletes waved their arms in jubilation at the most recent Olympic games, the camera almost always panned to their coaches, parents, teammates, or others who were the athlete's best supporters. No one succeeds alone. Great coaches help us perform better.

The lines between coaching and teaching, mentoring and supporting, and cheerleading and leading are blurred. Thankfully, good coaches do them all. The best coaches are concerned about both the *person* and the *performer*. They encourage the heart and know the race is against oneself, help us reach our full potential and are not satisfied until we do, and they care about us (not just the work) because they know that taking care of their performers is the best way to take care of the work. Many lesser managers will never grasp this concept. Employees feel better about the jobs they fulfill when they know their time, effort, and work are valued and appreciated, and they can bring their best selves to work every day.

Employee Engagement

Experts call employee engagement a discretionary effort. Employee engagement has been associated with higher productivity, better retention, and greater loyalty for employees, as well as an associated number of positive outcomes for the organization, such as higher customer satisfaction, higher revenue, and a better company reputation. Discretionary effort usually requires a psychological or emotional investment in the work; in short, the employees care enough about what they are doing to go above and beyond expectations and give it their all, regardless of what is required. Think of the employee who comes into the office on the weekend because she just wants things to be done right. Emotional investment in the work is not possible unless the employee feels the organization— through its supervisors, managers, leaders, and coworkers—reciprocates their care and concern. Great coaches help us believe in ourselves, our own potential, and the value of what we do. They boost our confidence.

An emerging wave of research demonstrates that employee engagement is as close to a holy grail as any other management concept. The idea is simple: employees who feel good not only about what they do, but also about their coworkers, manager, company, and overall work experience perform better than their counterparts. In short, great places to work create better performers. Employee opinion, satisfaction, and engagement surveys show a clear correlation between how employees feel, how they perform, and how their companies perform.

21ˢᵗ-Century Methods

How would one create a highly engaged workforce? One sure thing to do is to avoid poisoning the work environment and belittling employees with the antiquated management process called performance appraisals. Appraisals are 20ᵗʰ-century management technology and were created to supervise the labor of employees perceived as unmotivated, untrustworthy, and incapable of working independently. In the 21st century, we must have better tools to manage knowledge workers who have their own unique talent and expertise. They may work 24/7/365 from remote locations, have knowledge and skills that leaders do not possess, and are very capable of working independently. A new method of managing is necessary.

Questioning Paves the Way

The pioneering Performance Conversations method was designed for the modern workplace. There are three unique techniques highlighted in this book that will utilize this approach to performance improvement. Each orients itself toward the future, using inquiry, coaching, and a positive mindset to create conditions for success. Rich dialogue between the manager and employee stimulates the communication, cooperation, and collaboration necessary for the duo to produce outstanding performance and results together. Questions are utilized in this method to get the employee engaged in the conversation, take ownership of their work, and make decisions about what actions to take to improve performance. Independently, questions possess their own magic. They seem to empower people to think deeper, clearer, and more accurately, as well as to have greater confidence in what they know.

Questions also have tremendous utility and are everywhere. Wherever two or more human beings are gathered, questions are being asked and answered, in classrooms, boardrooms, living rooms, shop floors, stores, playgrounds, and workplaces, questions are being posed. They help us learn information, create new ideas, investigate issues, research scientific theories, solve problems, resolve conflicts, tell jokes, hire people, and are even used to bind couples together in marriage proposals and wedding vows.

It is almost impossible to communicate without the use of questions. They drive conversations, build relationships, and cause action. The magic and power of well-formulated questions can also be harnessed in the workplace to galvanize the performance of every employee. Managers must be able to use them effectively to be great managers and great coaches. Turn the page to learn how.

QUESTIONS

The Magic and Power of Questions

We learn more by looking for the answer to a question and not finding it than we do from learning the answer itself.
—Lloyd Alexander

Questions used effectively can unleash the potential of any employee. Like using the right key in a lock, asking the right question can open the door to unlimited possibilities. Questions can affect how people think, feel, act, and respond. Each question starts a journey, a discovery, a quest for truth, knowledge, understanding, and meaning. Every question holds a hidden mystery, a source of wonder, a sense of infinite promise in waiting.

Questions, it seems, have some sort of magical power that is not immediately obvious in their asking, but we all know they exist through our own personal experience. The right question asked at the right time can inspire, persuade, inform, insult, stop an argument, generate new ideas, solve problems, reveal motives, or cause action. Questions also possess the surprising ability to drive employee performance continuously upwards.

One of the secrets to better management and improved performance can be found in ancient wisdom. Socrates himself gave us the answer: the art of asking questions. Indeed, most advances in human knowledge, understanding, technology, science, and medicine have their roots in the scientific method—the simple, yet powerful, idea of asking and answering questions using specific protocols and techniques.

The art and science of asking questions
is the source of all knowledge.

—Thomas Berger

The power to question is the basis of all human progress.
—Indira Gandhi

Questions are useful for more than gathering information. In the workplace, questions can be used to improve the quality and quantity of work being performed. The Performance Conversations method is a new method of managing work that has the potential to boost every employee's performance by harnessing the power of inquiry.

As we will discover in the pages that follow, questions demand involvement, encourage interaction, engender engagement, build rapport, inspire ownership, and give employees a sense of control over their work. Every leader hopes for a breakthrough solution that drives individual performance and organizational results—asking the right performance questions may very well provide one of the keys necessary to achieving this goal.

Inquiry as a Management Art

Most professionals have a basic set of implements to use
in their craft. Carpenters have hammers, dentists have
picks, and physicians have stethoscopes. It is hard to
envision any of the people working in their chosen fields
without their basic set of tools. Managers, too, have a
basic set of tools: questions. And nothing is as simple, or as
complex, for a manager, or for any person in any position
of authority and responsibility, than asking questions.
—Terry J. Fadem[1]

Just as interview questions evaluate whether a candidate has the right knowledge, skills, and abilities to succeed in a job, performance questions ascertain to what degree an employee is succeeding in their specific role. While a question bank or a slate of tried-and-true questions can be used as a crutch when conducting an interview, the real art is the ability to develop the right question for the right purpose or specific job. The questions asked determine the answers received. The wrong questions could make poor candidates appear viable or fail to highlight the best candidate's skills.

Every manager must possess a basic set of skills to be successful, often including things like planning, organizing, writing, presenting, negotiating, delegating, researching, problem-solving, decision-making, and managing time. The skill of questioning—asking the right questions in the right way at the right time—should also rank highly on the list of required skills of any manager. This is because questioning is so vital to learning, understanding, gathering information, solving problems, and conducting quality control. They also encourage creativity, innovation, and ideation.

Knowing which questions to ask and how to ask them is an acquired and required skill for managers in the 21st century, principally because we work with knowledge workers who are intelligent and capable of independent performance. The role of the supervisor is to multiply an employee's effectiveness by providing the right guidance, support, direction, and encouragement. This means both parties must be constantly exchanging information, communicating, coordinating, and collaborating. Having a shared understanding of what is important, what needs to be done, and the proper plan of action is critical to success. Questioning is the best tool available for this vital information exchange.

Using proper lines of inquiry during a healthy conversation is a smart way to draw employees into a conversation and draw out the information necessary for success. This book will describe the art of asking questions and offer a framework for collaborating with employees to improve performance in most situations. It will also explain the Performance Conversations method, discuss how to gather and analyze key performance indicators, develop a set of seven key questions, and detail a way of accounting for and managing the most critical aspects of work through checklists. Finally, this text will provide instructions for developing and refining questions that can be tailored to one's unique work environment or employee group.

Unquestionable Value—Three Uses

The right questions alone can drive productivity; however, they are supercharged when systematized within the Performance Conversations method. As we will see, questioning is a basic skill that every manager must master. Therefore, the Performance Conversations Model deploys questioning in three different ways—the Performance Portfolio, Performance Questions, and Performance Conversations Checklist techniques. Each of these approaches will be detailed in the coming pages.

The Power of Questions

> *Driven by the belief that a question is more than the*
> *simple thing we might think it is—that, in fact, it's*
> *a unique instrument that we can get better at using*
> *if we try. Wielded with purpose and care, a question*
> *can become a sophisticated and potent tool to expand*
> *minds, inspire new ideas, and give us surprising power*
> *at moments when we might not believe we have any.*
>
> —Leon Neyfakh[2]

There are few verbal utterances as powerful as a well-placed question. They can be used to galvanize action, teach lessons, generate innovative ideas, solve problems, or simply make an emphatic point. Questions seem to have a weight that other forms of expression simply do not carry.

They can also open doors to information that may have remained secret. Since information is power, questions are a unique method of generating power. Questions help one control the dialogue in an easy manner. There is a Zen adage that "He, who forms the question, determines the answer." Using questions strategically is a hallmark skill of great salespeople and negotiators. Therapists use questions to uncover hidden motivators and inhibitors of behavior, while consultants use them to solve organizational problems that were previously out of their clients' reach.

> *My greatest strength as a consultant is to be*
> *ignorant and ask a few questions.*
>
> —Peter Drucker

Mediators use questions effectively to resolve conflict. People feel listened to when they are asked questions, and being heard is important to feeling appreciated and understood. These feelings pave the way to resolving differences.

Doctors use questions when making each and every diagnosis. Asking the wrong question could lead to a wrong diagnosis, inaccurate treatment, or even the demise of the patient. Lawyers make their case by questioning and cross-examining witnesses, while journalists use questions to report the truth. Questioning is an art mastered by the most successful litigators, police detectives, and investigators. One example is the almost mythological prowess of the television character Columbo, who would always prompt villains with "just one more question," usually the one question that undermined a previously ironclad alibi.

> *Accumulate learning by study, understand*
> *what you learn by questioning.*
> —Sha'n Master Ming Giao

In *Zen Lessons: The Art of Leadership*, Thomas Cleary references Sha'n Master Ming Giao's observation that questioning lies at the core of learning.[3] In their book, *Make Just One Change: Teach Students to Ask Their Own Questions*, authors Dan Rothstein and Luz Santana argue that empowering students to formulate and ask their own questions can transform the entire education process.[4] By asking questions, students learn better, discover meaning in their own way, and are empowered to continue their quest for knowledge. Anyone who has spent a day with a four- or five-year-old will know this to be true. Little kids ask questions incessantly —it is how they learn.

While seemingly simple, questions hold untold power. They can reframe situations and cause people to change, act, react, respond, think, and reflect. Their unique qualities can be harnessed to improve the performance of individual employees and their organizations.

What Are the Many Uses of Questions?

> *Learning to use the power of questions can dramatically*
> *increase your professional and personal effectiveness.*
> —Andrew Sobel and Jerold Panas[5]

Part of recognizing the power of questions is realizing their versatility. In business, questions can be used to gather information about the status of work being performed. A manager might probe staff for information to troubleshoot problems or clarify information for quality assurance. Questions can also be used to test employees' knowledge of rules, policies, or processes, notably during quiz-show-style training. This method can inspire a greater sense of accomplishment while learning and participating. Finally, questions can challenge research and development personnel to invent new products or services with a simple refrain like, "Is this the best product that we can create for our customers?" A well-placed question in the workplace can have a positive impact on the jobs being performed.

What Are the Many Types of Questions?

Experts have cataloged what seems to be an endless list of the different kinds of questions and their possible uses. While it may be important to know that different questions are used for various purposes and effects, it is not important to become an expert on the finer points of each type. Just as you can serve and enjoy great wines without a sophisticated knowledge of their history or the subtle flavors of their varietals, most managers will benefit from knowing just a few of the basic questions.

Closed-ended questions require brief, factual responses like "yes" or "no." Open-ended questions allow for an unlimited range of responses and are preferable in most circumstances where dialogue is important. Direct questions are clear, unambiguous, or blunt, and are used to evoke a specific response. Indirect questions, however, are inquisitive and do not have a conspicuous line or reasoning. Follow-up questions are used to clarify or expand a topic, and probing questions are useful for diving deeper into a topic or investigating an idea further. Leading questions can be used to corner a respondent into a narrow range of responses without their conscious knowledge. Trick questions are designed to manipulate a situation to the advantage of the questioner. While some questions may be more useful than others in a given circumstance, it is not necessary to master all of them or catalogue certain questions in one's mind for use at exactly the right moment. For most common purposes, good intentions and free flowing dialogue will allow all parties to find the prompts needed to communicate effectively.

We are constantly asking questions in our day-to-day lives, usually at the most basic level as we gather information. However, we must transform our use of questions on a conscious level and develop good questioning skills for use as a management tool. One good example of consciously using questions to manage more effectively is remembering to ask an open-ended instead of a closed-ended question. A manager could ask, "Did you forget to submit your monthly report again?," but a more useful question would be, "What is preventing you from completing your monthly reports in a timely fashion?" The former is a blunt instrument that could elicit defensiveness while the latter allows for stronger relationship building, troubleshooting, and information discovery that could lead to a novel solution or preventative measure. The subtle difference between these two approaches cannot be overemphasized. Mastering questions does not require advanced skill, but there are a few important protocols that enhance the use of questions, regardless of the type of question asked. This book delves into this subject.

Why Questions?

There are many performance management techniques used in organizations today. However, there are numerous research reports, anecdotes, and piles of evidence that have proven repeatedly what many of us already know intuitively—that performance appraisals as traditionally practiced do not work. There are countless horror stories of the bad ratings, bad meetings, bad decisions, embarrassingly long forms, poor supervisors, and other inept appraisal practices. The advice of an emerging army of experts is either to avoid them all together or to use an alternative approach to management. The Performance Conversations method is the best available alternative.

With this method, questions can be harnessed and channeled toward the goal of performance improvement. They can track, manage, and inspire employees in a better, smarter, and more effective manner. Questions also gather information about the quality and quantity of work being performed, like a normal performance review, but they have an advantage over other management techniques in that they have a list of positive byproducts. Some advantages are:

- stimulating dialogue,
- encouraging employee involvement,
- encouraging employee ownership of their work and the challenges associated with their work, and
- creating discovery and brainstorming opportunities.

As mentioned earlier, if questions can effectively determine whether a candidate in an interview can perform a job, questions should be equally effective in ensuring that the work being performed is actually meeting standards and expectations. Therefore, using questions within the Performance Conversations method is ideal for performance improvement. Additionally, the groundbreaking theory and practice of Appreciative Inquiry has proven for years that questions improve lives, communities, and organizations. Appreciative Inquiry is the art of asking questions to discover the highest potential of people and organizations. This approach has also been used for performance management and undergirds the Performance Conversations method.

What is the Basis of the Performance Questions Technique?

The Performance Questions technique is based upon the pioneering management method outlined in *Performance Conversations: An Alternative to Appraisal*. The design is simple: questions are used as a launch pad for deeper, richer discussions about the things that matter most in an organization. Questions are designed to enhance conversations about the work being performed with the singular goal of improving performance.

The Performance Conversations method is a performance improvement system—not a performance management system. It uses a coaching approach to supervision to help individuals learn, perform, and feel better about the work they do. The approach neither establishes a rating of performance, nor helps organizations make administrative decisions, such as who gets a raise or a promotion. It is not a backwards-looking exercise designed to document past efforts. Instead, it looks toward the future and focuses on better results.

The Performance Conversations method is based upon the idea that feedback and conversations, not appraisals or evaluations, are the pathways toward better performance outcomes. The premise is that performance is so dynamic that it cannot be managed once a year with a form completed during a single hour. Instead, the Performance Conversations method uses a structured feedback system that employs coaching techniques to optimize outcomes.

Holding conversations—not evaluations—is how people work together to find solutions to the most pressing challenges, uncover great new ideas, or create better ways of working. Conversation is the basic ingredient to communication, cooperation, collaboration, and coordination. Performance questions asked in the proper way and context provide the information necessary for making good decisions and acting affirmatively.

The Performance Conversations method is a structured approach to exchanging information with an employee through interactive dialogue, where the singular goal is enhancing their collective performance. Using dialogue and questioning ensures that all the priorities of the organization are wrapped within a simple package—brief, planned, frequent, and semi-formal conversation. It is neither an inquisition, nor an investigation; it is an active exchange and discovery process where both parties participate and ask questions.

Employee engagement is a constant theme in this book and a bedrock principle of the Performance Conversations method. Engagement starts by having employees create their own set of questions or ideas to ask or present to their manager during a 30-minute conversation. Appendix A provides example questions that employees can ask their supervisor to ensure that the conversation is productive from their point of view. The approach is designed to be semi-formal, and the questions asked respond to current challenges and opportunities in a free-flowing manner, whether using the classic Performance Portfolio technique or the newer Performance Questions or Performance Checklist techniques. These approaches focus on improving the most important aspects of work that are occurring today.

How to Ask?

> *What we know is that the need to be heard turns out to be one of the most powerful motivating forces in human nature. People want to be heard. Studies are quite clear that we care most about people who listen to us. People crave two things above all else. They seek appreciation and they want someone to listen to them.*
> —Andrew Sobel and Jerold Panas[6]

How one asks a question is just as important as the question itself. If a person is condescendingly asked twenty rapid-fire questions with a sense of entitlement to an answer, the respondent is sure to react with a bit of contempt. Such a power play rarely works. A humorous illustration might be a typical conversation between an overbearing father and his teenage daughter who has a part-time job, car, and an attitude. He may have the power, authority, responsibility, and prerogative to ask her any question he likes, but how he asks where she is going as she is headed for the door will make all the difference in the length and honesty of her answer.

The best advice on how to correctly ask a performance question is as simple as the idea of using questions in the first place—to ask genuinely and with good intentions. A supervisor who asks questions of their team in a manner that says, "I care about you and the work you do," and "I am concerned about the quality of the work that we perform together," will be highly successful and achieve what they intended. Think like a coach! They ask many questions with one goal in mind—gaining information that will eventually lead to better performance.

Is This an Interrogation?

A Performance Questions discussion should not be an interrogative exercise where an employee is battered with questions like a hostile witness. Instead, it should be two-way conversational dialogue. Employees will also be prepared with their own questions in advance of the meeting to guard against what could be perceived as an invasive procedure. They will be confidently ready for the conversation and will be empowered to fully participate, asking questions that lead to a shared understanding of the quality and quantity of the work performed.

Performance Questions are designed to be a starting point for dialogue about the most important aspects of an organization or workplace. There should not be any fear of asking the wrong questions or getting an incomplete answer. Questions are tools for conversation—a means to an end, not a conclusion. As long as the conversation elicits more or better information, the question asked is less important.

Because the goal of the conversation is to gain information in a casual manner, if there is ever a hint that an employee is starting to feel interrogated, the manager should stop asking questions and ask the employee to ask him or her questions. The employee will likely feel a sense of relief and a sense of control within the conversation. Additionally, using "we" instead of "you" in the performance conversation will help build rapport with team members and keep the general mood positive. Using "we" to talk about the work also implies that the employee is not in the game alone. It says, "You can do it, but I will help," and "You are responsible, but you are not alone." As noted above, the *how* you ask is as important as the *what* you ask. Genuinely asking questions with good intentions will go a long way in ensuring employees trust you to hear what they say and to work with them in achieving success.

What Forms Are Required?

There has never been a form that does all the things intended by most performance management systems, which is precisely why so many systems have exceedingly lengthy documentation. While four- or five-page forms are not uncommon, there are reports of forms that were thirty-four pages long once completed. Forms and bad systems fail for the same reason— they start with a preconceived notion of good performance. There is an assumption that the items on a three-year-old form work for every employee and kind of work. Forms create the illusion that only the things listed are the most important. This is hogwash.

Work evolves too quickly for a form to be effective. Priorities change, and an employee's need for support might vacillate due to their training, confidence, experience, or mood. What form could possibly adjust to the messiness of reality?

Therefore, avoid forms with dozens of performance measures, goal lists, professional development plans, comment spaces, and rating scales. Instead, use a simple form with the pertinent Performance Questions and a space for comments. Performance Questions are a simple and elegant solution to many performance challenges and opportunities. If a manager cultivates the right environment and asks free-form questions, the performance conversation (and future action) will naturally steer toward what matters most, what is happening now, and what needs improvement. Similarly, using a topic checklist to prompt conversation about the most important items in one's work and then reviewing the items together is a practical way of working. Success lies within the performance conversation itself, not on a form.

"Do You Have a Few Minutes?"—Thirty to Be Exact!

Each of the three Performance Conversations techniques requires only thirty minutes of the manager and employee's time, a few times a year. This is a small investment in future success, like a coach adjusting the game plan with the quarterback at halftime, or a ballet master encouraging the prima ballerina at intermission. Another situation could be a junior executive urgently calling a mentor about a workplace challenge. Each of these examples represent quick feedback sessions meant to keep the focus on outcomes, adjustments, or information sharing that might prove beneficial to future performance. All these situations could be enhanced and made more effective with a little structure from proven techniques.

A series of scheduled, thirty-minute conversations spaced throughout the year is the foundational element of the Performance Conversations method and will improve performance. An employee gets individual attention, reinforcement, direction, and support during these meetings, effectively creating a starting point for success. Google calls them one-on-ones, other companies call them check-ins, catch-ups, feedback sessions, touchpoints, snapshots, connects, performance talks, pep talks, progress reviews, or coaching conversations. Call them whatever works for your organization's culture, but plan and hold them as a means of improving performance.

A quarterly meeting is a mere two hours invested per year, bimonthly discussions would total three hours of time, and sessions scheduled every six weeks amounts to just four hours of time per year to ensure quality results. The frequency of meetings should be determined by assessing the type work being performed, the level of the employee's position, and the employee's record of success. Work with results produced over longer periods, employees in more senior positions, and more successful employees would dictate fewer conversations, just as work that is time sensitive, a junior employee, or a new employee would necessitate more frequent conversations.

Checking in at prescribed intervals ensures that performance is on track and stays that way. It provides a mechanism for adjustment, correction, reinforcement, troubleshooting, quality assurance, status reports, and information exchange. These information exchanges are the feedback opportunities that traditional performance management schemes say should happen continually throughout the year, but we all know that they do not normally occur in reality. The Performance Conversations method provides such structured opportunities. Questions are the tool of choice, whether using the Performance Portfolio approach and discussing evidence collected while working; the Performance Questions technique and asking tailored questions to drive improvement; or the Performance Conversations Checklist where a variety of management variables like recognition, career development, and retention are tracked and discussed.

PERFORMANCE CONVERSATIONS

Performance Conversations Theory and Practice

Theories, Models, Methods, and Techniques

Theories are overarching concepts that attempt to explain various phenomena and their interrelationships. Models describe a specific set of elements acting within a given theoretical context. Methods are processes or ways of interacting with given phenomena, and techniques show the practical application of such matters by putting ideas into practice. Experts explain the dynamic between these concepts through the theory to practice continuum.

The continuum explains how knowledge develops, how science advances, and how technologies are eventually applied to reality. For example, we once had a theory on how energy moves. We advanced by gradually harnessing energy, until finally we were able to use energy movement for our use by creating the technology for batteries. Management science works the same way. Great management practices first start with an idea, hypothesis, or theory, which eventually yields to a technique or way of working. Figure 2.1 offers an approximate representation of these concepts as applied to performance improvement.

Performance Conversations in Theory

Four theoretical underpinnings converge to create the Performance Conversations working method. *Conversations, Not Evaluations* presents the idea that dialogue is the best way to solve problems and unleash human potential. This is in stark contrast to traditional appraisals that assume ratings and judgments improve performance. *Positive Psychology* is the study of what makes humans thrive. Performance improvement—getting,

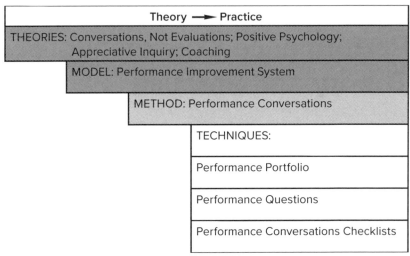

Figure 2.1. The Theory to Practice Continuum

doing, and feeling better—parallels the Positive Psychology concept of flourishing. *Appreciative Inquiry* is the art and practice of asking questions to uncover and discover the highest potential of people and organizations. *Coaching* is helping individuals enhance themselves and their future goals.

All four theories are aimed at improvement, which is why the Performance Conversations method is a performance improvement system and not a performance evaluation process. A summary of these ideas is offered below.

Conversations, Not Evaluations—The Theory

The *Conversations, Not Evaluations* hypothesis argues that the best way to achieve a resolution between two opposing parties in international diplomacy, legal matters, marital or interpersonal conflicts, or any other potentially intractable disagreement is engaging in frequent and earnest two-way dialogue. The workplace is not any different. Solving workplace challenges does not allow for ratings or waiting until the end of the year to address an issue. Positive intent, rapport, and open communication are all main ideas of this hypothesis.

The alternative to such conversations is destructive situations, like conflict, war, lawsuits, or broken hearts. Traditional appraisals do not encourage open conversations or healthy debate because they are too focused on delivering judgement and justifying the power held by a supervisor. When used to determine raises, it is clear that the communications are not conversations at all—they are a play-acting dance with a predetermined end.

It should not need further justification, but communication and conversations are what make us unique from other species and form the basis of the human experience. Good communication is also the hallmark of great relationships and helps us solve problems, plan, coordinate, and build rapport.

Positive Psychology—Theoretical Elements

While the Positive Psychology field of study has only been recognized as a science since 1998, its foundational ideas are as old as humankind itself. What makes for a "good life"? What conditions help humans thrive? Father of Positive Psychology, Marty Seligman's shorthand for well-being and happiness is PERMA: positive emotions, engagement, relationships, meaning, and accomplishments. It would not require careful study to see the parallels with these and the Performance Conversations method.

People want to feel proud about their work and accomplishments, and they want to have good relationships with family, friends, and coworkers. Employees thrive at work when they are engaged and their work is meaningful and fruitful. The Performance Conversations method is positivity-oriented by design. The first question that is often asked in this approach is, "What is going well?"

Other questions that track closely with the positive emotions (P), relationships (R), and accomplishments (A) aspects of the PERMA model are "How are you?," "How are your professional relationships?," and "What is the status of your goals?" Creating the space for earnest two-way dialogue and asking questions like "What else is going on?" imply a search for information, meaning (M), and understanding. Requiring employees to ask their manager questions not only demands employee participation, but also creates a forum where interaction is expected and desirable. Involvement breeds engagement (E). It almost seems like the Magnificent Seven Questions of the Performance Questions technique (to be introduced later) were designed to support human thriving and Positive Psychology concepts…maybe because they were.

The premise of Positive Psychology—flourishing—explains why the science is so powerful and how it relates directly to the Performance Conversations model. Like traditional medicine that once almost exclusively focused on curing physical disease, traditional psychology focuses on human functioning disorders with the goal of treatment. However, the focus in the 21st century is on what makes people thrive: positive psychology; the health movement in modern medicine; and performance conversations that help people get, do, and feel better about their work. The search is underway for methods of accentuating and building upon one's strengths, not documenting failures or establishing ratings.

Positive Psychology and Its Application to Management

One of the first introductions of Positive Psychology to management theory and practice was Marcus Buckingham's bestselling book, *Now, Discover Your Strengths*. However, management practice has been slow to adopt this amazing practice—we are still stuck in 20th-century thinking. The deficit-thinking behind finding and shoring up the gap between desired outcomes and actual performance sounds so intuitive that it has been the dominant theory of management practice for as long as anyone can remember. The problem is that it is probably just wrong. This idea works well for machines, but humans are not that simple.

Positive Psychology seeks to discover what makes humans thrive, flourish, create, prosper, and feel emotionally healthy. Traditional management practices ask the opposite question. Positive Psychology and its building block concepts (like Appreciative Inquiry) have repeatedly produced extraordinary results in the laboratory and reality. Why, then, are we still using old management science and tearing people down in the annual performance appraisal process? Despite all the advances in science that Positive Psychology offers (a treatise on it is beyond the scope of this book), the simple conclusion that building upon one's strengths produces better outcomes than shoring up one's deficits has not been widely adopted. One cannot make elephants fly. We should ultimately be trying to help people be their best now and in the future and stop trying to get people to be who they were not meant to be.

All of us are great at some things and less gifted at others. Some of us are artists and athletes, while others are born to be accountants and actuaries. The likelihood that an artist's lackluster appraisal will cause an epiphany for him to become an expert in completing detailed expense reports is much lower than it would be for him to code an app (application) to avoid many of its steps. The former works against his disposition while the latter taps into his creativity. Performance appraisals would rate him low on his administrative acumen, but a Performance Conversation would identify his interest, passion, and creativity and channel it toward finding a solution to his lackluster completion of paperwork.

Positive Psychology and Appreciative Inquiry seek what is possible and what is positive. They tap into the unlimited human potential to create, thrive, build, seek, and innovate. Unlike appraisals, they also build upon strengths and do not focus on deficits or gaps.

Positive Questions Lead to Positive Change

The statement that "Positive questions lead to positive change"[7] should not need any scientific proof to be confirmed. This Appreciative Inquiry approach tells its own story. "Why did you do that?" versus "What circumstances caused you to do that?" yields dramatically different responses from a teenager (don't ask me how I know this). The leader of a 327-year-old institution in Virginia prefers the question "How might we?" to help it overcome its history of being apprehensive about change. There is magic in these three words. They communicate so much with so little.

"How might we?" is simultaneously encouraging and empowering. It creates its own unlimited possibilities. It removes pessimism organically and overcomes opposition without even acknowledging its presence. When followed by the word "imagine," it transforms yet again. "How might we imagine a world where _____ exists, and how can we go build it?"

Traditional appraisals ask the wrong questions, if they ask any at all. The questions posed are often used to lay blame, justify a rating, or serve as a departure point for correction. Positive questions do not tear down before attempting to build one up again, although it is unlikely that this even possible in the time and space immediately following supposed "constructive criticism."

The question, "Think about yourself at the beginning of the year and the person you are today. How have you changed?," would not be asked during a normal appraisal. Think of the conversational possibilities with one's employees if questions are posed differently and founded upon good intent. We know how harmful and ineffective it is for people to feel fear before an appraisal because they expect to hear critical feedback, but the value of positivity is just as intuitive.

Appreciative Inquiry—Theoretical Elements

> *Appreciative Inquiry is about the search for the best in people, their organizations, and the relevant world around them. In its broadest focus, it involves systematic discovery of what gives 'life' to a living system when they are most alive, most effective, and most constructively capable in economic, ecological, and human terms. Appreciative Inquiry involves, in a central way, the art and practice of asking questions that strengthen a system's capacity to apprehend, anticipate, and heighten positive potential in a way that is grounded in affirmation and appreciation.*
>
> —Patricia Burgin[8]

Appreciative Inquiry (AI) uses questions to discover and unleash potential, not to focus on problems. Its name is descriptive. First, it acknowledges and affirms the value of something (a person, company, community, etc.) and appreciates them. Next, AI searches for that thing's greatest assets to enable it to get better. In short, AI seeks to uncover or discover its greatest potential.

The purpose of this book is to help one get better, work better, and feel better. Asking questions is a fine art; AI makes them purposeful by focusing on the future and its possibilities. AI theory includes models and methods, one of which is the Initiate, Inquire, Imagine, and Innovate framework. Another description of the AI method is the Discover, Dream, Design, and Deliver approach. Nevertheless, the quest is directed toward excellence and positive questioning is the best tool.

Coaching as a Theory

Everyone knows the difference between a coach and a boss. Today, people hire life coaches, executive coaches, and personal trainers to help them get better physically, mentally, or emotionally. The theoretical ideas behind coaching include orienting toward the future, improving, developing, and curating one's best self as both a person and performer. The metaphors surrounding a boss, manager, or supervisor, however, are less than flattering. Coaching is different in its idea, intent, and practice. A *relationship* is warmly developed with the coach, while a boss-employee arrangement is only designed to facilitate work.

The irony is that coaches are sometimes demanding, uncompromising, loud, aggressive, emotional, mercurial, and maybe even rude when working with others. Yet, it is the intent that matters. Coaches want us to get better for our own good; managers want us to get better so that we can work better for the organization. However, there is nothing forbidding the average manager from developing a coaching relationship with his or her staff. Note that appraisals do not help grow this relationship because the manager is put into the position of a judge, not a trusted partner.

Some might argue that the differences between coaching and managing are mere semantics. A closer investigation will yield the truth of the essence, ideas, foundational beliefs, and advantages of coaching. These coaching concepts, orientations, and theories yield results very different from the practices and techniques used with management. Table 2.1 summarizes some of the major differences between a supervisor, coach, mentor, and sponsor.

Is Coaching 21st-Century Management?

In the 21st century, a great deal of work is performed by knowledge workers—experts in their own right. The need for supervision is not the same as it was fifty years ago when managers were knowledge workers and most staff members simply provided labor. Today we need coaches, not overseers who ensure people come to the office and work for a set number of hours. Employees now work with a variety of tools in totally different ways, scattered across time zones and places. They work with technologies, not physical instruments. Therefore, our approach to supervision should be just as fluid and capable as our employees and workplaces.

Coaching is a process of helping others grow, develop, prepare, and perform. A supportive supervisor focuses on the employee and what the employee needs to perform. This individualized attention enables employees to reach their unlimited potential through a shared commitment—a partnership.

Mentors and Sponsors

Mentoring is an advanced form of coaching where a coach takes a personal interest in the success of someone else. The mentor provides advice on both work and personal matters to support the whole person, not just the employee. Good mentors give advice in the gray areas of work, such

Table 2.1. Coaching Continuum of Support

← Continuum of Support →			
Supervising	**Coaching**	**Mentoring**	**Sponsoring**
Monitoring	Helping	Guiding	Advocating
Managing	Supporting	Encouraging	Enabling
Watching	Caring	Protecting	Promoting
Employee works for Manager	Employee works with Manager	Manager works "for" Employee	Manager works on behalf of Employee
Training	Developing	Challenging	Inspiring
Drawing out	Investing	Advising	Counseling
Motivating	Inspiring	Strengthening	Championing
Authority	Partner	Sponsor	Representative (Agent)
Supervisor	Mentor	Role Model	Benefactor
Performs separately	Performs together	Manager provides exposure	Manager provides opportunities
Work relationship	Personal relationship	Confidant	Trusted Partner

as maintaining professional etiquette, recognizing the unwritten rules of success in an organization, making introductions to build one's network, as well as other tips that are not usually written down or widely known. Like superior performance, someone becoming a mentor is a result of discretionary effort. Employees are fortunate when their manager *chooses* to extend beyond the obligations of work and take a personal interest in them.

A sponsor is further down the continuum of support. A sponsor is an advocate that looks for or identifies opportunities for the employee, removes obstacles, or solicits opportunities to give to the employee so that they are more successful. They provide references, write recommendations for awards, and request that other leaders place the employee into stretch assignments, special projects, or leadership development opportunities. They go beyond what is expected and often go to bat on the employee's behalf.

A 21ST-Century Management Model
The Rich Fabric Created by Four Complementary Theories

Various parts of this text might seem repetitive because Appreciative Inquiry, Positive Psychology, and coaching are interrelated theories that focus on the same thing—improvement. Their intersections create the fabric that makes the performance conversations approach so strong. Their foci are slightly different, giving the model breadth, but their commonalities form a strong core. The *Conversations, Not Evaluations* theory applies these ideas in a workplace performance improvement context and provides a solid foundation for a new management practice. Together, they create a modern and effective system for managing performance in the 21st century.

A Final Critique—Down with Appraisals

> *Performance appraisals wouldn't be the least popular practice in business, as they're widely believed to be, if something weren't fundamentally wrong with them.*
> —Peter Cappelli and Anna Tavis[9]

A final critique against traditional performance appraisals should not have to be made in this day and age. Nearly everyone who has ever held a job knows appraisals do not work. However, for thoroughness's sake, a brief critique is offered here.

Designed to Fail: Appraisals Do Not Work

> *...the biggest limitation of annual reviews—and, we have observed, the main reason more and more companies are dropping them—is this: With their heavy emphasis on financial rewards and punishments and their end-of-year structure, they hold people accountable for past behaviors at the expense of improving current performance and grooming talent for the future, both of which are critical for organizations' long-term survival.*
> —Peter Cappelli and Anna Tavis[10]

The *Harvard Business Review* article "How to Give Feedback to People Who Cry, Yell, or Get Defensive" offers sage advice for difficult situations or performance reviews.[11] However, the article does miss a few essential points. First, performance appraisals by design are flawed and self-defeating. The artificial environment where one expects to hear negative feedback prompts, primes, and programs employees to come ready to react. Second, the relationship matters. If an employee and a manager have a great relationship and a history of mutual respect, the employee is less likely to react. A troubled history, however, will affect what is said regardless of how skillfully it is delivered. This is the main point: no manager possesses enough skill to overcome the fallacies upon which traditional appraisals are built.

The mere publishing of an article called "How to Give Feedback to People Who Cry, Yell, or Get Defensive" tells us all that we need to know about traditional appraisal systems. We know they generate and inflict harm. They were not designed to work.

Managers Are Set Up for Failure

> *Feedback can, and sometimes should, be tough to hear. However, if an employee feels demotivated, criticized, disappointed, or depressed after a feedback session with their boss, the manager failed.*
> — Cheyna Brower and Nate Dvorak[12]

According to Gallup's 2018 Workplace Experiences Panel Survey, almost 90% of employees are actively disengaged or not engaged after receiving negative feedback. Within that 90%, almost 30% are actively looking for employment elsewhere and over 50% are passively looking for other employment. There is nearly fifty years of evidence that shows how traditional appraisals and negative feedback are destructive to relationships and employment. It is a wonder that people continue to use them.

We No Longer Sell Them, Nor Do We Buy That Appraisals Work

The list of notable organizations that have abandoned traditional performance appraisals is impressive. In the October 2016 edition of the

Harvard Business Review, human resources gurus Peter Cappelli and Anna Tavis dubbed these moves part of the Performance Management Revolution.[13] The companies that have announced they have abandoned appraisals include Adobe, Cargill, Colorcon, Dell, Expedia Group, The Gap, General Electric, IBM, Kelly Services, KPMG, Lear Corporation, Medtronic, Microsoft, OppenheimerFunds, and SAP. Even the professional services firms who previously sold such systems to the world have abandoned them, including Accenture, Deloitte, and PwC. If the leading drug companies said they were no longer selling a specific medicine because they themselves learned it was ineffective, most people would believe them and stop using it as well. The days have come and gone for traditional appraisals.

Similarly, even the software companies that automate old processes have abandoned them. The head of HR for SAP SuccessFactors noted, "Grading workers did not work. People are open to feedback, also to harsh criticism, until the moment you start giving scores. Then the shutters go down."[14] Experts have concluded what science has already proven—people want conversations, not evaluations. For the past seventy years, baby boomers have tolerated performance appraisals, but millennials have outright rejected them.

Millennials: A Special Case Argument Against Appraisals

> *Continuous feedback isn't just a pushback against the obvious shortcomings of annual reviews, like the fact that they are infrequent and unpopular. It's a product of social and mobile tech which makes it easier than ever to give in-the-moment responses and share insights with any co-worker at any time; millennials in particular want and expect that level of feedback.*
>
> —Workpop[15]

Even General Electric acknowledged that part of the reason they abandoned traditional appraisals was that they did not work for the millennial generation. (They did not work for previous generations either, but that is beside the point.) Millennials have different ways of thinking, relating, and working, all of which are inconsistent with traditional appraisals.

Like previous generations, millennials find appraisals off-putting. Studies have also shown that, like their forbearers, millennials start looking for a new job after a negative experience during a traditional appraisal.[16] However, unlike other groups, they will start looking for a job fifteen minutes after negative, so-called constructive criticism is delivered. Additionally, a sizeable percentage (22%) of millennials report having called in sick to avoid an appraisal.[17] Their reactions are telling—millennials have different expectations for work.

What Millennials Want Related to Performance Management

The secret? Consistency. Whether a millennial
employee's work product is excellent or poor, if
you wait a year to give constructive feedback or
recognize good work, you're going to lose them.
—Tom Gimbel[18]

The differences between baby boomers, millennials, and Generation Z is talked about in almost every workplace breakroom, reported on by nearly every news outlet, and is often the subject of humor on every television network. The differences between the generations are legendary. With millennials having recently surpassed baby boomers as the largest generation working, their peculiarities are no longer a laughing matter. The workplace must now adjust to them.

The rough summary below was compiled from a series of studies and white papers on millennials and shows their views on matters relating to performance management. They seek:

- Regular communication
- Candor
- Transparency in decision making
- Involvement in decisions affecting them
- Continuous and precise qualitative feedback
- No ratings
- Genuine, authentic interactions
- Coaching-type management
- Recognition

- Opportunities to learn and advance
- Meaningful work
- Freedom or flexibility in work assignments

Did I mention recognition and encouragement? Millennials' needs and desires for work are different. However, their expressed interests are wholly reasonable, desirable, and worth pursuing. Baby boomers lived during a different time where the relationship with supervisors, managers, and organizations was much more deferential, hierarchical, power-based, and paternal. Things no longer operate that way. Instead, we now work in flat, matrixed, fast-paced, communicative, and evolving organizations. We expect to hear from our CEO often, not just once a year during the holidays. Some expect to hear from their supervisor every day. Many boomers might associate going to the boss' office with going to the principal's office. For the millennial, however, it might be analogous to going to a trusted friend's home.

Millennials Want a Lot of Feedback

> *Be a coach first, manager second: For many millennials,*
> *ongoing consultation is not a sign of weakness, but*
> *rather a real-time feedback loop used to self-correct.*
> *Managers should be willing to grant millennials this*
> *informal access, serving as regular sounding boards and*
> *providing younger colleagues with valuable perspective.*
> —Deloitte[19]

A popular television commercial tells the story of the legendary neediness of millennial employees in contrast to baby boomers. The setting is an interview with an older gentleman and a younger man. As the millennial finishes answering a question, the bored baby boomer gets a text alert. He looks at his phone and it is from the millennial sitting across the table from him asking, "How did I do?" As a baby boomer author, I am still laughing. Millennials prefer a great deal more interaction with, and feedback from, their managers. Annual feedback sessions that were the norm for baby boomers will not work for the new generation.

Some of the literature on feedback for millennials sounds more like a pattern found in text messages. They want short, factual, precise messages delivered frequently. While performance improvement messages may not be limited by characters, the idea of feedback that is accurate, timely, and brief is a pretty good one.

A Coach Needed, a Boss Not Wanted

Millennials want and need more support, instruction, and encouragement than their predecessors. This is not all bad. They appreciate the Performance Conversations notion of co-performance where the employee is in a partnership with the manager. They see work as a collaborative and shared responsibility. Managers of millennials will need to be cheerleaders, or active supporters who continuously root for their player from the sideline while the game is in action. Waiting until the end of the game (or the end of the year appraisal) to offer praise and support is simply too late.

Millennials Do Not Like Ratings

Millennials prefer qualitative over quantitative feedback. Numerical ratings, made famous by companies like General Electric (GE), are not appealing to this new, dynamic generation. In fact, even GE has overhauled its performance management system and removed performance ratings.[20]

Millennials were born into an instant feedback and on-demand world and they want continuous engagement with the situations and people around them. They ask questions, lots of questions. They will not passively accept a 4.5 rating, and they will ask questions not to challenge, but to understand. These questions will likely undermine the supposed indefatigable truth ratings claim to uphold. They might ask: "What does a 4.5 really mean?" "Is a 4.5 really fair?" "What do I have to do to get a 5.0?" "Who else got a 4.5?" "Did I get a 4.5 because of that one assignment and the missed deadline?" "Do I have to be perfect to get a 4.75?"

The truth is that numerical ratings approximate many factors that the average manager cannot explain or justify, even if they want to. Millennials want precise, open, clear, honest, and accurate feedback and information, and they want it often. So, while very few baby boomers were willing to challenge their managers, millennials will push back. Traditional appraisals were not built for them.

Millennials Want Performance Conversations

If millennials want regular, ongoing communications; involvement and engagement in their work; authentic interactions with their manager; support; coaching; encouragement; and feedback, they want to participate in Performance Conversations, not evaluations. If the method had not already been invented in 2006, we would have to accommodate the group that now represents over half of today's workforce. The Performance Conversations method has come of age at the right time—along with the millennial generation.

The Performance Improvement System

The Performance Improvement System consists of five elements that reinforce one another and make the best use of several proven management techniques to enhance growth, rapport, and results. This system focuses on the future and is goal-oriented by design. Regardless of whether performance is poor, average, or exceptional, the system seeks to enhance all work execution. It is relentlessly optimistic.

Feedback, feedforward, frequency, follow-up, and familiarity are the five principles of the Performance Improvement System. Feedback is specific information received in response to previous actions. Feedforward is a forecast of preferred future outcomes. Frequency is efforts taken over time. Follow-up is reengagement to ensure completion. Familiarity is about relationships and context. Together, these five factors are used to coach employees to optimal performance, outcomes, and impact. Figure 3.1 is a helpful graphic for understanding their connections.

The Fabulous Five: Feedback, Feedforward, Frequency, Follow-up, and Familiarity

Feedback and feedforward are about the exchange of information, or communications. Frequency establishes intentional, ongoing interactions used to track and manage work. Follow-up ensures things get done, adjusted, or intentionally abandoned. More holistically, it is accountability. Familiarity creates an open, comfortable bond that makes communication, interaction, and future difficulty easier to handle. It also enhances potential outcomes due to a partnership mindset.

Each of the elements of the Performance Improvement System and model reinforce one another and are integral to how and why the Performance Conversations method is a superior approach to managing and improving employee productivity. The elements are synergistic. Feedback and feedforward work together as they bridge what has happened, what is occurring, and what can be done. This continuity ensures that the things that have slipped offtrack are adjusted and monitored. Things that are going well are replicated. Everything else is evaluated for potential intervention.

Frequency provides the opportunity to monitor things and keep the momentum. Follow-up is the flipside of frequency and serves as a tracking mechanism. It also supports the building of rapport and familiarity. This makes follow-ups easier because participants are already acquainted and know what to expect of each other. The intersection and integration of the five elements of the Performance Conversations Performance Improvement System help to create its magic. The system does not work because of any one element, but because the whole is greater than the sum of the parts. These proven management practices have molded together to form a more superior whole.

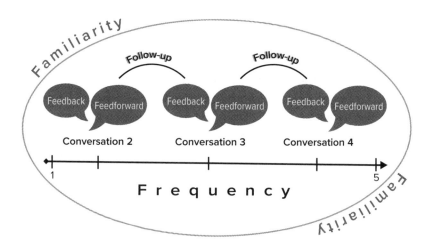

Figure 3.1. The Fabulous Five: Performance Improvement System

Familiarity

Familiarity: The GAPING Hole in All of Performance Management Literature
Familiarity exposes the largest hole in all of performance management literature. Performance appraisals are fraught with problems, but the one that is most overlooked and unacknowledged is the impact of a supervisor and employee's relationship. It matters!

People are unlikely to heed the cautions and warnings of people they do not like or respect, no matter how wise the advice. No reasonable person wants to interact with their adversaries. Most sports teams would not accept tips from their opponents. Competitors in business do not openly share information with each other. Few countries seek the counsel of their enemies. Relationships matter.

When people do not trust their manager, there is nothing that can be said in an appraisal that will be heard or valued. Even if a manager tells an employee they did a fantastic job and will get a 20% pay increase, the employee will feign excitement and say to friends, "We will wait and see if it actually hits my paycheck. I just don't trust him." The reaction would be even more cautious if it were a promise of a 20% increase in the future if their performance measured up.

What happens when employees think their manager does not like them? Employees will not receive feedback in the manner intended if they feel the manager plays favorites, does not come around enough, acts forgetful, nitpicks, behaves discriminatorily, or possesses an assortment of unhelpful or unhealthy views. The accuracy of the information and the skill with which it is delivered are irrelevant. Relationships matter.

Anyone with more than one sibling, friend, or colleague knows that the same information, delivered the same way, at the same time from two different people communicates different information. The history and experience we have with people color the way feedback is received. This truism cannot be discounted, dismissed, or overstated.

The Relationship Changes the Feedback

The relationship governs an interaction even before actual work is discussed. How is it possible that management literature has ignored this basic reality of human interaction for the last seventy years? We know about the halo effect, the primacy-recency effect, and we are trained to focus on the performance behavior and not on the person. We know to be timely and specific, and we are aware of the countless other supposed truths about giving good feedback. Yet, managers have never been told or trained on how their familiarity, respect, fondness, dislike, preference, or style of interaction with employees will elevate, enhance, undermine, distort, or generally influence what happens during a performance discussion. The messenger sometimes becomes the message.

The Performance Conversations model acknowledges this irrefutable truth and attempts to address it in the most productive way possible. The model builds relationship and rapport cultivating elements into the framework, as well as some accountabilities for keeping both parties honest. These and other elements of the model and its context will be discussed in the pages that follow.

Feedback

The concept of feedback hardly needs explanation due to its ubiquity in management literature. It is information provided in response to actions and events. Its goals are perfectly aligned with the goals of the Performance Conversations method: to determine what has gone well so that it can be replicated, to identify what has not gone well so that it can be corrected, and to gather information that can be utilized later for preventing problems or seizing opportunities. The machine metaphor works well to describe feedback. After inputs are collected and processed, the resulting feedback is used to determine the next step. A manager might inform an employee that her projects are always completed on time and on budget but could use some more creativity. Additionally, through dialogue, she learns that no other team member has completed all their projects on time. She then knows that she has exceeded the standard but can take a little more time to give things pizazz. She uses the information received to adjust.

Feedback Is Not Appraisal

Feedback can get a bad rap, but it is information while appraisal is judgment. Nothing could ever be made or improved without feedback, whether it is positive, negative, or neutral. Every natural and manmade system relies on four elements: input, process, output, and feedback. If the outputs are good, the process repeats. If the outputs are bad, an adjustment is made. If they are neutral, an investigation is conducted to reach a determination. In an office setting, feedback is used to make the work better. It is also complementary to the next principle, feedforward.

Feedforward

> *When correctly implemented, the rather simple one-to-one and collective communication feed forward competency has proven to be a very powerful, strategic change-management tool. In short, the capacity to feed forward can quite successfully help create important and sustainable individual and collective changes in perspectives. It can usefully be implemented in problem solving, in conflict resolution, in training and consulting, in personnel evaluations, in project management, as a systematic meeting process in teams, etc.*
>
> —Metasysteme[21]

Feedforward Is Anticipatory Adjustment

Feedforward requires feedback to make changes within a system so that performance is improved. A modern thermostat is a great example of a feedforward system. If the desired temperature for a room is 72 degrees Fahrenheit, an older thermostat will use feedback and turn on the heat or air conditioning when the temperature goes down or up a couple degrees. The temperature will always be within 70–74 degrees. Newer thermostats notice smaller changes in temperature and adjust the heat and air conditioning sooner. More importantly, they also anticipate temperature changes and provide more heat or AC before the temperature change is noticeable. Using the Internet, they monitor the outside temperature and anticipate changes to the internal temperature, adjusting before or just as changes are necessary.

The cruise control in a car is another example of a feedforward system. The car knows that its speed will slow going up hills and increase going down hills, so the system adjusts in advance of a full hill so that the speed of the car remains fairly constant. Feedforward systems anticipate changes and adjust before or during the process, while feedback adjusts only afterwards. Ultimately, feedforward uses feedback contemporaneously.

Today's smartphones and artificial intelligences are also proving to be great feedforward systems. A smartphone learns a person's patterns and sends them a coupon for their favorite restaurant or suggests a new one based upon their preferred cuisine. It can also alert someone in the morning that his or her commute will be slower due to traffic. This feedforward mechanism uses previous feedback to forecast what is likely to happen.

Coaches who learn the patterns of their players and tell them what to do before a common problem is encountered utilize feedforward. A tennis coach might ask her players to mentally adjust to prevent errors on the court or improve future performance. Feedforward is also useful with actions we already perform well. Telling a player that her backhand is her strength and she should maneuver to put herself into position to use it more is feedforward. It describes or imagines a future outcome and engages the performer in using their skills and wits to bring it to life.

A supervisor might know that one team member works well under pressure while another does not. Her feedforward conversations with the two would be tailored to their needs. One might be required to submit a timetable for his work so that he does not get overwhelmed and bow to the deadline, while the other might just be reminded of the project's importance. In either case, feedforward learns and gathers information (feedback) and puts it to use proactively.

Feedforward minimizes unwanted variances in a system or machine and the performance of a person, team, or organization. Feedforward is about efficiency and effectiveness as much as it is about preventing or reducing errors and margins of error. More importantly, it maximizes potential outcomes by constantly adjusting, calibrating, and recalibrating responses to get to an idealized future state. Feedback is as purposeful as it is responsive.

Feedforward Is Coaching

> *Feedforward coaching focuses on goals, not standards.*
> *The manager and direct report work together to identify*
> *goals that are specific to the individual's role and aligned*

to corporate objectives. This is critical as it guarantees that workers will know 'what is expected of me,' which is another key driver of engagement and performance. It also frames the conversation in a meaningful way. Are the goals on track or not? Why? What can the individual do to improve? What can others do to support?

—Kevin Kruse, 2012[22]

Feedforward in the Performance Conversations approach obligates the manager to help the employee succeed; that is, to be a good coach. One of the questions is, "What can I do to help you perform at your highest level?" The supervisor then becomes accountable for the results of the employee's collective efforts or collective lack of effort. This is the essence of the notion of co-performance. The coach only wins when the employee wins.

Coaching is an interactive process that is future and improvement oriented. Feedforward is a coaching partnership where the manager and performer discuss, describe, and agree upon future outcomes, then work together to achieve those goals. This partnership creates the space for good rapport and a mutually beneficial relationship.

Feedforward Performance Conversations

Whether performance has been on the mark, below par, or neutral, feedforward takes that information and uses it for improvement. It focuses on questions like "What if?", "What's possible?", and "How can we use this information to…?" Feedforward is a vital component of the Performance Improvement System as it is focused on future possibilities.

Feedforward is not a Pollyanna approach that avoids negativity. By design, feedforward requires feedback, so negative information cannot be avoided. Instead of making a conclusion or judgement about problems, however, feedforward gives employees the chance to minimize its impact. In traditional appraisals, feedback is a conclusion. When things do not go well, feedback can be used only to justify a rating. Feedforward says, things did not go well and "How do you think things will improve if we were to try this?" The emphasis is on the future, which takes the sting out of things that cannot be changed.

When married with feedback and frequency, feedforward is provided while the game is still being played. The frequent, brief, structured check-ins in the Performance Conversations Model provide for adjustments while they can still affect the outcome. Feedback delivered at the end of the year or game is almost useless; feedback provided at halftime is useful. Coupled with feedforward, feedback is impactful, but feedback can just be critical and judgmental without it. Feedback is static, historical information or measurements. Feedforward is active and coaching, and, overall, an improvement technique.

Feedback and Feedforward Comparisons, Contrasts, and Complements
According to the One-Minute Manager®, "feedback is the breakfast of champions," therefore feedforward would have to be the protein of performance. It tells one where to go, what to seek, and inspires action. Feedback and feedforward are complements, with neither as useful without the other, and together they are very impactful. Table 3.1 provides some useful comparisons and juxtapositions of the concepts:

Table 3.1. Feedback and Feedforward: Comparisons, Contrasts, and Complements

Feedback	Feedforward
Comparisons, Contrasts, and Complements	
Information	Aspiration
Objective	Optimistic
Evidence	Imagination
Reflective	Prospective
Accuracy-oriented	Improvement-oriented
Problem identification	Solution identification
Diagnosis	Action
Confirming	Affirming
Positive and Negative	Positive
Standards	Goals
Educating	Empowering
Encourages participation	Encourages partnership
Encourages/Discourages communication	Encourages communications/ Collaboration
Subject to overgeneralizations	Requires specificity
Hierarchical, Senior-Junior	Nonhierarchical, Supporter-Supported

Feedback is sometimes perceived to be bad in the management literature because it is incorrectly mistaken to be synonymous with appraisals. Feedback is information; appraisals are judgment. Even negative, critical, direct, and biting feedback can be received in a good light if the intent, context, and delivery is appropriate. Coaches give biting feedback all the time, sometimes even with expletives. However, the context and intent are different from feedback from bosses. The coach is usually trying to help us get better and improve our own performance. Negative feedback from coaches is perceived differently than negative feedback from bosses because it is usually combined with feedforward. It is a "Don't do that anymore, do this instead" proposition instead of a "Let's document this incident for the record" occasion. In a traditional appraisal setting, negative feedback is given about the game that just ended.

Everyone assumes coaches have positive intent, but why? It is the relationship because relationships matter. It is the context because the game is being played and players still have a chance for a good outcome. Additionally, coaching is delivered in practice and before the game, when time is taken to help players get better. Feedback without feedforward is incomplete and ineffectual. It is more important to tell someone what to do that is good than what not to do that is bad.

Perhaps this analogy is not befitting the circumstance, but it is descriptive. Telling a child to stop playing with his food at the dinner table is folly. This is what kids do—they play. It is far more productive to tell him to take two bites of potato. Telling an employee that you have identified four patterns of mistakes in her business reports is valuable and indispensable for her improvement. Yet, telling her will not improve her performance if she does not know how to make the changes. One must first describe or deal with the issue at hand and then forecast and direct the future outcome. Identifying solutions is as important as identifying the problems they solve. Feedback and feedforward are complements and they synergistically reinforce one another.

Feedforward and Questions

> *We live in worlds our questions create.*
> —David Cooperrider[23]

As noted, the elements of the Performance Improvement System are self-reinforcing. Feedforward makes ample use of the art of asking questions. Indeed, asking provocative questions that inspire dreams, actions, and initiatives is probably the only way to produce breakthrough results. Ordinary results are attainable by many means, but extraordinary results usually start with provocative questions. Such stimulating thoughts are sometimes as simple as "Why?" or "Why not?" Tantalizing phrasings like "Wouldn't it be cool if we could…?" or "Can you imagine what would happen if we produced…?" and "What would a _____ have to look like to make our competitor's customers switch to our brand?" are also useful.

Nonetheless, questions are a foundational feedforward technique. It is hard to think of a feedforward conversation that did not utilize questions to engage employees in finding solutions or designing successes. Here are some examples of feedforward questions:

- What did you learn from the mistake with _____ that we could put to good use?
- What can we do differently next time?
- What are the areas where you think you have the most to learn?
- What do you think are the areas where you can benefit the most by asking for help from others?
- What are you most excited about in your work in the coming months?
- What can we do together to help you excel?
- What conditions do we need to create to help you perform at your peak?
- How did the problems with _____ help you think differently about your assignments?
- Do you know what you did to create such as a fabulous solution (so you know when and how to do that again)?
- How can we focus more on _____ in the future so that we accomplish our goals faster?
- How do you feel about your work at this point in time?
- Would it be okay if we _____ next time?
- In the future, how should we try to account for all the variables before we start the project?
- Is it okay with you if we…?

- Can you tell me about a situation where you thought you were off-track but continued forward anyway?
- Can you imagine...?

All of the above questions can be used to correct poor performance. The approach is different from making accusations of poor performance or calling attention to past misgivings. Instead of highlighting that an employee is not engaged, or does not like some of their work, one could ask, "What are you most excited about in your work in the coming months?" The manager could then note that the responses are misaligned with the highest priorities of work. This will lead to a discussion of adjustment.

"How did the problems with _____ help you think differently about your assignments?" is far superior to saying, "You screwed up and what are you going to do about it?" Similarly, saying, "In the future, how should we try to account for all of the variables before we start the project?" is better than saying, "You don't pay attention to details and therefore your projects veer off course and require rework." The former empowers the employee to own the problem and determine future actions. The latter lays blame, causes defensiveness, and does not help determine the best path forward.

The examples of feedforward provided above primarily focus on resolving problems intentionally instead of discussing easy or neutral subjects. They make the point that feedforward techniques are not only happy-go-lucky quips, but also hard-core accountability tools. Managers tend to shy away from accountability questions because they are hard, but positive questions about producing exciting things are far easier to draft. We do not avoid them here.

Feedforward and Appreciative Inquiry

At the core of Appreciative Inquiry is the notion that by eliciting stories of success, one can identify patterns that could support future high performance. Appreciative Inquiry has been applied to a variety of contexts, including developing leadership capacity and imagining possibilities in organizations, and improving personal relationships.[24] Kluger and Nir have applied Appreciative Inquiry to the performance management process by developing the feedforward interview methodology.[25]

Simply using the one-word question "Imagine?" invokes the effects of Appreciative Inquiry, therefore feedforward is both a coaching and an Appreciative Inquiry technique. Both focus on the future and seek to improve current situations or practices. They are designed to encourage ownership of one's circumstances and possible solutions. Most importantly, they are derived from one's strengths. Both Appreciative Inquiry and feedforward seek to build upon the strengths of a living system—a person, an organization, or a community. They both focus on resolving problems by focusing on the possibilities.

Feedforward Builds Rapport & Relationships

*The benefits of FFI appear to include eliciting positive
emotions, fostering bonding, building psychological
safety for sharing information, and creating internal
transformations of both interviewer and interviewee.*

—Kluger and Nir[26]

The Feedforward Interview (FFI), as described by Avraham Kluger and Dina Nir in the *Human Resource Management Review*, is a performance discussion which uses Appreciative Inquiry techniques, not the normal appraisal, to uncover stories about performance.[27] The results of their study are impressive and are foundational to performance management in the 21st century. Almost all new methods of performance management involve a periodic, one-on-one interview with questions and discussions to build rapport and discuss ways of improving, not rate performance. Later studies have validated the findings first introduced by Kluger and Nir.

Feedforward Works

Most of us would not need scientific proof that feedforward works, but scientific validation is nice, nonetheless. Similarly, no one needs to read countless studies to know that traditional appraisals do not work, for we have all experienced the resulting fear, injustice, and bias. From study to study, traditional appraisals are universally disliked. No one needs to be a scholar to want to do something different.

With a focus shifting away from old ways of working to new methods, emerging evidence validates what we already know: feedforward works. Authors of an article in *Human Resource Management* found that employees who received a feedforward performance review performed "significantly better on the job four months later" than employees who participated in traditional appraisals.[28] Other studies have shown positive effects between feedforward and the building of interpersonal relationships, motivation, communication, and performance improvement.[29]

Aside from the impressive array of evidence mounting in management literature, there are countless studies in classroom settings that show feedforward-related techniques working. There are considerably more feedforward studies in the educational field because these techniques are more prevalently used and advanced—think about teachers giving students feedback and feedforward on their academic assignments. One can guess how the results differ between appreciative, strengthening, forward-looking questions, and blunt feedback, criticism, poor grades, and admonishment. It is intuitively smarter to use feedforward techniques with young people who have not yet learned what to do differently.

As noted, these ideas should not need evidence. We already know that the criticism, labeling, judgment, and negativity found in normal appraisals and evaluations cause students, professionals, friends, and family to recoil. An argument that positive sentiment, support, encouragement, and optimism are ineffective at helping people improve does not even seem plausible. The real question is why have we relied on appraisals for seventy years and failed to adopt feedforward as our default way of working?

Frequency

> *On average, only 15% of employees who work for a manager who does not meet with them regularly are engaged; managers who regularly meet with their employees almost tripled that level of engagement.*
> —Annamarie Mann and Ryan Darby[30]

Frequency—Because Work is Ongoing

Frequency is a simple idea, but it is harder to do than it first appears. It requires a pause in the action; it is a time-out, an intermission, a break. The tempo and demands of work make taking a break and having a discussion on how things are going seem like a distraction. A salesperson might ask,

"Do I have to stop making money to talk with you this afternoon?" A manufacturer might count the minutes of lost productivity, and a computer programmer might argue that she is involved in a detailed and complicated problem-solving task and does not want to lose her train of thought. These are precisely the problems that frequency is designed to solve.

Tomorrow's sales are in jeopardy when we are working and our results are getting increasingly diminishing returns. Our first tendency is just to work harder. A manufacturer might argue that an engineer's time is better spent evaluating production numbers; however, that is until mistakes are found in the design or production improvements are missed. Computer programmers everywhere seem to prefer coding over meetings, but many might leave their organization because their tasks have become repetitive and boring. When would a manager learn that a person is no longer feeling valued or challenged? A good time for resolving these potential issues is during a performance conversation.

Frequency Builds Discipline

> *Excellence is an art won by training and habituation:*
> *we do not act rightly because we have virtue or*
> *excellence, but we rather have these because we have*
> *acted rightly; 'these virtues are formed in man by*
> *his doing the actions'; we are what we repeatedly*
> *do. Excellence, then, is not an act but a habit.*
>
> —Aristotle

Frequency builds routines, routines build habits, and habits lead to excellence. Planned and scheduled meetings assure that necessary things are addressed in a timely manner. Problems cannot fester. The discipline to follow the schedule has its own reward. As the saying goes, "Bad news does not get better with age." Quarterly performance conversations allow for difficult discussions and keeps them from being delayed or avoided. An employee is obligated to disclose concerns when the manager asks, "What is not going well?"

Similarly, if the manager has noticed things are out of kilter, she has the venue to discuss those observations. The occasion can be used to review data, reports, patterns, or other activity, and the discussion is usually fruitful. Asking "What else is going on?" is an opportunity to find improvements, remove obstacles to success, or brainstorm possibilities. The planned frequency of performance meetings allows for discovery, decision-making, adjustments, and (of course) accountability.

Frequency Ensures Accountability

Frequency guarantees accountability. Managers are notorious for avoiding difficult conversations because confronting people or sharing tough news is hard. However, a manager has no excuse for delaying negative feedback when a discussion is already scheduled. This is also good for the employee because they will know they cannot be set up to fail by the manager holding back negative feedback until it is too late.

Additionally, everyone gets busy and distracted with too much on their plate. Things change, as do priorities. While everyone knows ongoing feedback is necessary, making time to actually exchange it is a challenge. However, when meetings are planned and scheduled, everyone works toward it as a built-in deadline. An employee trying to postpone a performance conversation is a warning signal to the leader. A manager who cancels too many meetings with an employee is being negligent. Frequency demands that *the things that matter most* have a prescribed time and place to be discussed.

"What is not going well?" is softened when asked after "What is going well?" because it is expected; however, it is no less potent. It is the ultimate accountability question, as an employee cannot hide from unattractive data or information. It would be willful neglect to not tell the boss that one is two months behind on a project but disclose the next month that he is now three months behind. You cannot be three months behind today if you were not two months behind last month. Frequency holds both the manager and employee accountable for doing the things that need to be done—discussing challenges and finding opportunities for improvement.

How Frequent is Frequent?

The optimal frequency for performance conversations is best determined by evaluating the work being performed and the characteristics of the individuals involved. Feedback should be delivered in a timeframe closest to the work performed and with enough time for potential adjustments. Work in the retail industry could be seasonal, consulting tends to be project-based, public works might be planned over years, and computing hardware and software projects have varying timelines. Semiannual meetings make no sense for medicine where quarterly adjustments might be necessary based on new technologies entering the field. Some businesses might find monthly meetings to be too disruptive and time consuming. However, they may be productive and transformative for a retail establishment with rampant turnover due to competition in the local job market.

New employees should have more sessions with their manager so that they can become acclimated to their organization, department, manager, and work. Though the organization may only require quarterly performance conversations, the new employee might meet with his manager every month for the first four months and then join the regular departmental schedule.

Organizations might mandate a minimum of two check-ins a year, divisions may require quarterly sessions, and an individual manager in the same organization might choose to hold bimonthly sessions based upon the work requirements in her department. The organization may want to ensure clear job requirements, aligned strategic goals, and career development annually. A divisional vice president may be concerned about quarterly goals, turnover, and employee engagement. The director may want to ensure that employees feel supported, engaged, and that their learning and performance goals are met. All of these and more can be easily accomplished with the Performance Conversations method.

A manager can send a calendar invite to direct reports inviting them to a thirty-minute meeting on a Wednesday morning once every eight weeks. Nothing more needs to be done. The best part is that periodic meetings can be set far in advance with any calendar application. Meetings that conflict with emerging situations can be postponed a few days or cancelled when appropriate, but the event reminder keeps both parties honest. It ensures that time is reserved in advance for important conversations.

Experience shows that quarterly conversations are the standard. Trimester meetings are also a sound option. New employees or departments with junior staff may prefer pep talks every six weeks. Academics might hold meetings once per semester and once in the summer. Overall, performance conversations should be scheduled every four to sixteen weeks to be effective.

Special Circumstances and Frequency

If an organization makes big changes or moves in a new strategic direction, it may take some time, training, and lots of coaching for employees to become comfortable working in the new method. This is a great opportunity to use the Performance Conversations method to advance organizational goals. Adding a special coaching conversation or check-in to every employee's schedule could be one way of reinforcing the strategic change. The same goes for inserting an item into the Performance Conversations Checklist or a new question onto a Performance Questions slate, such as, "Can you tell me how you understand how your work is affected by the company's new strategic plan?" Adjusting the schedule of conversations is natural and easy in the Performance Conversations method because the goal is improvement on the things that matter most. When things change, the process adapts.

Frequency—Meetings on Request

No one would choose to add an additional performance appraisal meeting because appraisals are not designed to be positive experiences. However, when the focus is on conversation and improvement instead of ratings or evaluations, it is common for employees to solicit more feedback. This is an easy adjustment with the Performance Conversations method. An employee who is struggling, who wants more support and coaching, or who has exciting information to share might request holding the next conversation earlier or scheduling an additional time. This is desirable and reflects a healthy work environment. It communicates that an employee has a good relationship with their manager and trusts that the meeting will be helpful to both them and their work.

Follow-Up

Follow-up is organically built into the Performance Conversations method due to its sister element of frequency. The opportunity for follow-up exists but effort must be made. Prescribed conversational items must be discussed, goals must be deliberately tracked, efforts must be monitored, and the status of projects requiring continuity must be updated. The process facilitates follow-up when planned, periodic meetings are already scheduled.

Some topics are worthy of repeated discussion. That is, every conversation should be focused on the highest work priorities and the status of efforts in those areas. This is good follow-up, and these ends can be met using the Magnificent Seven Questions (to be discussed later). Similarly, a checklist approach (also to be covered later) keeps the conversational focus on important matters: situations going well, not going well, and other useful status updates.

Follow-Up Is Management at Its Core

Management requires giving direction, checking to see if guidance was followed as intended, and ensuring outcomes meet expectations. The quality control inherent to management is impossible without follow-up. Anyone can tell someone what to do, but ensuring that things are actually done correctly is the minimal expectation of supervision. Therefore, follow-up is management.

Telling someone what went well (feedback) and discussing what could be done differently (feedforward) is important and effective, but expecting behavior and efforts to change without follow-up is folly. This is made worse if the follow-up occurs months later, or worse yet, at the end of the performance cycle almost a year down the line. Coaching, supporting, redirecting, calibrating, and recalibrating is necessary for optimal performance. Follow-up is a management tool used by successful managers.

Follow-Up Builds Trust (and Relationships)

Frequency and follow-up are accountability measures, but they can also build confidence and trust. An employee interested in becoming promotable by learning new techniques will be surprised and delighted if the boss gives him a flyer about a relevant certification course as a follow-up from their last conversation. Employees feel confident that their leader is interested in them and their work when they follow through with their promises. The best couples, teams, groups, and organizations place a high value on trust. Some experts argue that trust is the number one factor that distinguishes successful organizations.[31]

David Horsager, expert behind the Trust Edge Leadership Institute, mentions many elements in his book, *The 8 Pillars of Trust*, that are reinforced organically in the Performance Improvement Model, specifically the clarity, compassion, commitment, and consistency pillars. Clarity comes from repeated communications and inquiry. Exchanging information and questioning is at the root of performance conversations. Coaching builds compassion because coaches are concerned about improvement in both the person and their performance. Follow-up breeds commitment. Staying steadfast along with someone during a difficult situation is appreciated and shows both compassion and commitment. Frequency and follow-up are two sides of the same coin as they collectively communicate commitment and consistency. The Performance Improvement Model of the Performance Conversations method builds rapport and trust without even trying.

Trust is built is ancient wisdom. *Trust cannot be given; it is earned* is another axiom. Things are built one brick at a time. Follow-up allows for the placement of a few stones at each meeting. A pile will accumulate, giving the employee more confidence in the relationship and the opportunity to establish better rapport with their leader. Their beliefs and investment in the relationship will get stronger not only from more interactions, but also from more follow-through. The more one commits and accomplishes, the more others will believe in them. This is true in any relationship— supervisor-staff relationships are no exception.

Follow-Up and Homework

The frequent nature of one-on-one conversations maintains momentum and the rhythm of progress. One cannot put off responsibilities when the next performance conversation is in a mere five to six weeks. If improvements need to be made, research needs to be conducted, or changes in practice undertaken before the next conversation, it is best to start now— immediately after the performance conversation meeting. Frequency discourages procrastination and encourages action. The gentle deadlines baked into the Performance Conversations method ensure starting homework early.

Follow-up Closes the Loop

Things that are going well are reinforced and replicated when discussed at successive meetings. Situations that are not going well are tracked, corrected, or adjusted at meetings until resolved. Moments that were cautions or concerns in the last discussion are investigated, and both parties discuss if their troubleshooting activity worked in the next conversation. Potential opportunities are exploited by follow-up: "The last time we met you suggested we analyze our cancellations to see if there was a pattern. You will be delighted to hear that I found out it is mostly with new subscribers who haven't fully learned the benefits of our products. Good job, that was a great suggestion."

Follow-up seems rather obvious and mundane, but it is a basic ingredient in good management. However, everyone gets busy and forgets the little things, the pace of work does not always allow for celebrating successes, and the to-do list seems to grow instead of shrink. Follow-up built into the process creates a nice crutch for managers who have more to do than time will allow. It helps everyone stay honest. We have already discussed that follow-up helps the growth of rapport and trust because it shows proof. Trust is built when one is found to follow through, over and over again.

Follow-Up in the Performance Conversations Method

In the Performance Portfolio technique, a meeting summary lists the things that must be tracked or followed up on in one page or less. Bringing this note to the next meeting keeps each party honest. In the Performance Questions technique, there is a question dedicated to the status of goals, plans, and follow-up items, so it goes without saying that follow-up is managed. Depending upon the items chosen for discussion on a Performance Conversations Checklist, a placeholder for follow-up items can be included as a useful prompt. However, in all cases, some way of thinking about and tracking those items which require continuity can be accomplished effortlessly in the Performance Conversation approach. The beauty of this is that good management is baked into the model without the need for different protocols for tracking and managing productivity.

From Improvement Model to Improvement Method

There are likely dozens of ways to use the Fabulous Five Performance Improvement System to increase or enhance the productivity of people in many walks of life, sports, or workplaces. Feedback is information used to assess one's productive location. Feedforward is forecasting and planning to improve. Frequency provides continuity of thought and effort, and follow-up ensures things get completed. Familiarity brings a partnership to the performance.

Imagine getting feedback on one's workout routine from a personal trainer. She identifies one's strengths and needs and offers a prescription in the form of a new regimen. She outlines a new schedule to follow, and then she checks in three times a week to see how things are going. If a day or two is skipped, she will call and meet you in the gym. On the days you are in the gym, she checks your progress from the intervening days and monitors you while you work out. Her relationship to you is instructor, taskmaster, cheerleader, and encourager.

A would-be entrepreneur gets a retired executive to provide him with feedback on his business proposal. The analysis yields some promising and problematic elements. The executive suggests they meet each week for a few months to discuss the finer points and the refinement of the proposal. Each week the executive offers suggestions, guidance, and some to-do items for the next meeting. When the entrepreneur gets discouraged, off-track, or attempts to delay meetings, the executive challenges him to "stick with it" and focus. Over time, the entrepreneur begins to learn the discipline and self-motivation necessary to forging a new venture. He also begins to appreciate the mentorship and friendship provided by the retired executive.

The Performance Improvement System—feedback, feedforward, frequency, follow-up, and familiarity—is obviously at play in these two examples and can be used to enhance the productivity of nearly every employee at work, and in nearly every role available in the 21st century. The system will be employed within the Performance Conversations method in the pages that follow.

The Performance Conversations Method and Techniques

The Performance Conversations method is a performance improvement system by design. It is built upon the idea that feedback, not appraisal, produces better productivity. The Performance Conversations method provides both the tools and the opportunities for managers and employees to collaborate and produce excellent outcomes. This is accomplished through a series of structured discussions surrounding the highest priorities of work. Traditional performance management systems are designed to document and rate past performance with the false notion that this motivates employees to perform better.

Traditional performance management systems have at least three elements: a design framework, instruments or tools, and a meeting between the manager and employee. The design frameworks vary and include rating systems, narratives, 360° feedback models, individual development plans, competency rubrics, goal-setting approaches, or some combination of these designs. The instruments used are usually forms with rating sheets, tracking devices, comment sections, or skill inventory lists. Each system then requires a meeting between the supervisor and employee where the manager delivers a rating or results to the employee. The Performance Conversations method turns traditional systems on their head. The focus of this pioneering approach is on the dialogue itself.

The only way performance improves is through feedback, feedforward, and agreement. Employees exchange information with the supervisor, receive feedback on how their performance compares to standards and expectations, and are given guidance, direction, support and encouragement to get better. It is imperative that the conversation ends in an agreement on the main points and future actions. Feedback is information and diagnosis, feedforward is guidance and forecasting, and good management provides direction, support, and encouragement. An overarching generic label for these collective activities is coaching.

The Performance Conversations method provides a structured approach to such information exchanges and multiple opportunities to coach employees to higher performance. The employee shares responsibility for the feedback session and his or her own performance outcomes. Their involvement ensures optimal results during the conversation and eventually in the workplace. The focus of these discussions is performance improvement, not ratings.

An Overview of the Performance Conversations Method

In order to improve employee productivity, the Performance Conversations method utilizes the following elements:

- Brief, structured, planned, periodic conversations
- Interactive, question-based dialogue
- Orientation toward the future and improvement
- Coaching and co-performance concepts
- A holistic approach to improvement, including efforts, outcomes, and behaviors

Brief, Structured, Planned, Periodic Conversations

Performance conversations are designed to be semiformal, thirty-minute conversations regarding the things that matter most in one's work and work environment. They are formal because they are structured, planned, and frequent. They are informal because there is a free-flowing and two-way exchange of information. The dialogue unfolds based upon the needs of the work and the people involved. Since the goal of the meeting is to help the employee improve performance, he or she is a full participant in the dialogue. Structure is provided by the topics of conversation. Conversations are always planned and specifically focused on the highest work priorities. They are scheduled in advance and recur every four to sixteen weeks, depending upon the local circumstances, work, work environment, and people involved. This provides for continuity, ongoing feedback and feedforward, and good management.

Interactive, Question-Based Dialogue

Since performance conversations meetings are designed to help an employee learn, perform, and feel better about their work, the employee must be a participant—not a passenger—in the discussion. Employees are trained to come prepared to a performance conversations meeting, and they are usually armed with good questions. Preparations can be required and asking questions should be expected, ensuring employee engagement. If employees are unable to discuss their work, it is unlikely they understand it and will be able to perform and improve it. The model helps the employees by giving them the tools necessary for participation.

Orientation toward the Future and Improvement

The focus is on the future, as the past is not subject to change. Feedback is used as input into the feedforward process. Feedforward is designed to forecast what actions can be taken for improvement. There is a positive, upbeat, future-focus to a performance conversation. Therefore, don't use ratings, as they are meaningless and ineffective at preparing one for future performance. The focus is on what the employee and their manager can do to work together and produce better outcomes.

Coaching and Co-performance Concepts

Coaching focuses on both the person and the performer. The coach-performer bond is built through steady encouragement and collaboration. Coaching implies a relationship; the coach only wins if the employee wins, too. The athletic metaphor is most illustrative here. In no sport can a coach win and player lose—they co-perform. This reality cannot and does not apply to the workplace, but it should.

A Holistic Approach to Improvement, Including Efforts, Outcomes, and Behaviors

Performance Conversations focus on the whole system. It accounts for learning, performing, and engagement—getting, doing, and feeling. Therefore, it is concerned about the person and the performer. Similarly, it has a holistic work perspective. One's actions, methods, and ability to follow instructions are integral to producing quality work. Outcomes, results, and impacts are necessary measurements for success; nevertheless, they are insufficient. Behaviors color everything we do in a human enterprise. Does someone work well with others, is he inclusive, or is he a destructive force that drags down the entire team? One's efforts are the building blocks that produce outcomes, and one's attitudes and behaviors either fuel or inhibit greatness.

The elements of the Performance Conversations method are designed to specifically focus on the most important things about work and find avenues for improvement. Conversation, communication, and collaboration are at the core of the approach. The performer and coach collaborate to build a better understanding and produce improved outcomes. Some tools help them organize their effort, like logs, portfolios, and structured meetings. Regardless of the details, it is not a complicated process but a planned, structured, and periodic conversation regarding things we find most important. In summary, the model has the employee and manager come together for thirty minutes and complete the following:

- Agree upon the most important priorities of work and their levers
- Discuss these matters
- Ask each other questions
- Diagnose problems, correct them, and attempt to prevent them from happening again
- Identify good outcomes
- Try to replicate these outcomes as they look toward the future
- Recognize or reward good outcomes
- Share information
  › to identify potential problems or obstacles,
  › to identify opportunities for improvement, and
  › to check-in and see if the performer is doing well.

Without any training, preparation, tools, or support, all the manager and employee have to do is think about and focus on the core elements of the work and then plan a series of meetings for discussion. At its essence, the model is a two-way, interactive dialogue which uses questions to stimulate collaborative problem solving, coordination, and improvement planning.

The Performance Portfolio Technique

The book *Performance Conversations: An Alternative to Appraisals* introduced the Performance Portfolio technique. A detailed outline of the approach is provided in those pages; here, we will simply summarize the highlights. Many of its core elements were detailed above as well because (like the Performance Question and Performance Conversations Checklist techniques) it is built upon the Performance Conversations method, or a series of brief, structured, planned, and periodic conversations about the highest work priorities. In this case, however, both the manager and employee are armed at their meeting with a great deal of evidence from an electronic file or physical portfolio.

Collecting Evidence for Discussion, Diagnosis, and Decision-Making

The Performance Portfolio technique is organized by a system that tracks and collects evidence of work for future discussion, diagnosis, and decision-making. The three elements that put the technique into action are *performance logs*, a *portfolio* to gather the logs and other evidence of work, and a *progress review* meeting. An annual summary meeting is expected, though not required in this technique.

Both the employee and manager keep notes about anything that has occurred over the previous period in separate quasi-activity logs. Only the most noteworthy actions, activities, events, observations, examples, samples, or other work outcomes should be logged. When the manager and employee meet for their periodic check-in, they discuss the collected information and what it reveals about the employee's performance over the interim period. They then determine the next steps. The collected evidence (e.g. copies, reports, photographs, awards, complaints, and performance logs) helps them diagnose problems, replicate successes, and exchange observations that might be helpful for the future.

Performance Logs and Portfolios

There are many ways of tracking notable performance indicators. The best tool is one that reflects the work being performed and the people documenting it. A manager might keep a supervisor's journal or notebook and make notes throughout the quarter. A marketing professional might keep track of things in a spreadsheet. Some people prefer to keep notes on a paper calendar as this makes it easier than having another tool to manage. Clever younger people might keep notes in their smartphones or take pictures to document all their efforts. The method of tracking performance can and will vary, the only requirement is to populate a log with notes and observations, and keep a folder of samples, examples, and other artifacts of work that are worthy of discussion.

Reviewing the Evidence

The collection of evidence and artifacts can be kept in a paper or electronic portfolio, and an online folder on a shared network drive works just as well as manila folders. The two logs and evidence from each party creates a great show-and-tell opportunity for comparing and contrasting notes. The differences are especially valuable as they call attention to divergent viewpoints and priorities which should be reconciled. Clarity supports and agreement improves performance. When the employee and manager track different things, the manager can refocus their attention or praise the employee for taking the initiative to handle important matters for which the manager was unaware. The evidence of good work makes it easier to conduct interactive performance conversations.

Performance Portfolio and Questions

Like all Performance Conversations, questions drive the dialogue. Questions ensure that employees participate and that managers communicate expectations, feedback, and direction. The Performance Portfolio technique introduced three essential questions that should be asked in any and every performance conversation regarding employee improvement:

1. What is going well, and how can we replicate it?
2. What is not going well, and how can we adjust?
3. What else is going on that may help us identify, prevent, or solve problems, or seize available opportunities?

These questions are also used in the Performance Questions technique and can be discussed in the Performance Conversations Checklist technique for those wise enough to consider them. Here, with the Performance Portfolio approach, improvements are confidently made because they are based upon a collection of evidence. Table 4.1 compares different ways of asking the three essential questions foundational to the Performance Conversations method.

Table 4.1. Three Essential Performance Conversations Questions: Alternative Phrasings

1	What is going well?	What are two things I should continue doing?	What are areas where we have our greatest successes?	Where are we being most successful, and why?
2	What is not going well?	What are two things I should stop doing?	What are the inhibitors to success?	What should we change to make things more successful?
3	What else is going on?	What are two things I should start doing?	Where are our greatest challenges and biggest opportunities?	What are two things that concern you, and what are two ideas that we should pursue?

The intent of the three essential Performance Conversations questions is to help the employee understand what it takes to produce and reproduce success, independently troubleshoot, identify and prevent potential problems, and share improvement ideas with their manager. The questions' phrasing and the manager's and employee's work methods are flexible as questions are generally adjustable to the local style of thinking and working.

Performance Conversations: Examples in Action

While the Performance Conversations method was designed with office-based professionals in mind, it can be adapted to almost any work environment with a goal of performance improvement. The standard thirty-minute coaching conversation may not be suited to every setting, yet the principles that support the model still apply. Feedback, feedforward, frequency, follow-up, and familiarity can be the Holy Grail of effective management for all occasions. Having periodic discussions focused on the most important work aspects is the other half of the solution. The examples that follow provide five different instances of this method at work in unique environments.

Trip Reports as Performance Conversations

A business that provides terrestrial maps to miners and government agencies adapted the Performance Conversations method to follow their work. Employees would conduct multi-week expeditions to remote areas carrying sophisticated mapping equipment. The hundreds of miles trek back seemed to take longer than going and was usually filled with idle chatter, relaxation, or boredom. So, instead of waiting to return home to debrief and complete paperwork, performance conversations were held during these rides. The team leader would isolate him or herself with one team member at a time and discuss what went well, what did not go well, and otherwise exchange pertinent information about the employee's wellbeing and work. These so called "Trip Reports" were recorded and sent to the administrative staff back at the office to transcribe.

Upon their return, the employee and supervisor could review, correct, amend, or endorse the Trip Report. This interpretation of the process fit well with the work performed and did not require additional scheduling, planning, forms, or work. Feedback was timely and immediately used to discuss future trip improvements. The feedback and feedforward were discussed in the most realistic context—on the trip. Frequency was ensured as the team met at the conclusion of every expedition. Follow-up occurred while giving feedback or signing the Trip Report back at the office as the team leader reflected upon the implementation or lack of adjustment from previous advice or suggestions. The relationship, or familiarity, was built with each interaction, provided that both parties acted in good faith and worked together to make each expedition more successful than the previous one.

Far, Far Away—Performance Conversations with Remote Workers

Remote workers are becoming more prevalent, but the performance management literature seems to ignore this population and their coaching, which often means tracking, monitoring, managing, and assessing their work from afar. One team of *Fortune* 500 remote workers held monthly check-in telephone conversations with their team leader. Members met biannually as a group and saw their leader and each other irregularly when they completed projects together in different cities. It is hard to feel like one is part of a group when you only see your teammates less than forty days a year.

Weekly conversations with the manager and e-mails are great for completing the work, but it does not take care of the professional or the work on a macro level. The monthly check-in conversations filled this void. Sometimes they were filled with casual small talk about the kids and family or the little annoyances of biweekly travel. Nonetheless, this seemingly idle chatter allowed the leader to get to know the people she supervised and build rapport. It was also a retention tool. Knowing how important family was to certain employees allowed the leader to uniquely schedule travel to respect their priorities. She knew that most employees who had ever quit her team were those who could not balance remote work, frequent travel, and family matters. Those who built support systems were more successful.

Planned monthly performance conversations in this environment helped build familiarity and rapport. The conversations were structured to make sure that both feedback and feedforward were provided. Staff members appreciated the dedicated time and attention from their leader. While most of the conversations were held over the phone, some were conducted through videoconference. The Performance Conversations Model allows for such flexibility.

Giving Voice to Colleagues—Performance Conversations at Universities

The concept of shared governance is embedded in colleges and universities, meaning that faculty and staff can participate in institutional decision-making. Therefore, most employees feel empowered to participate on committees and task forces. Experts say that employee involvement is one of the biggest variables in employee engagement and organizational success; colleges and universities provide such opportunities in abundance. Some say it is "making every voice heard." While not the case in everything, employees have the opportunity to provide input into major decisions.

Higher education environments in the United States, Canada, Australia, and South Africa have adapted the Performance Conversations method. The technique is attractive because it is an interactive exchange of information and employees help interpret the evidence collected about their performance. These characteristics acknowledge the values that many members of higher education communities hold true. They belong to such environments because they believe in collegiality, consensus building, respect for an individual's talents and abilities, contributions, and service to something greater.

It would be antithetical to the environment to have a single manager act as the sole arbiter of an individual's worth and contributions during an appraisal. It just seems odd that one person would have the corner on knowledge, truth, and alleged facts and evidence. Academics like to debate, and there would be endless arguments about what a 4.5 rating actually means. Can it be measured, quantified, and validated? Such debates are avoided when a respectful work dialogue is used instead of traditional appraisals and ratings.

(The poetic irony of the Performance Conversations method is that it was born from ideas advanced by Don Harward, the sixth president of Bates College in Maine. He offered his community a quarterly discussion called the Conversations Document. His ideas were prescient.)

Did the Bread Rise at the End of the Day?— A Unique Performance Conversation

A bakery in the South held five-minute, stand-up performance conversations every two or three weeks with its line work employees. It was an industrial bakery where an individual's performance success was obvious at around 2:30 p.m. every day. If the bread did not rise, the employee's performance that day was subpar.

The environment was hot and required hard, detailed work. The wages reflected the hourly labor market, and turnover was the enemy. Employees could potentially leave and work for another organization for fifty to sixty more cents per hour. The time it took to replace a staff member and train the new hire on the fine art of bread baking was debilitating to the business. The turnover monster was tamed through performance conversations.

The shift leader would carry a clipboard with a three-question survey and pull three to four employees off the line each day between 4:30 and 5:00 p.m. The meeting was held standing up in a corner near the work environment. The leader checked in with each selected staff member to see how they were doing and if they had any questions or concerns. Some employees required interpreters to communicate with their leader. Regardless, the periodic conversations were short, planned, and focused on the most important things about work. Was the work being done in the right way? Was the employee okay with the work and environment? Could the supervisor do anything to help the employee be successful? Was there anything else the employee wanted to talk about? Employees knew they would have dedicated time with the supervisor every few weeks. This alone helped reduce turnover as it gave employees an opportunity to discuss concerns and the supervisor time to intervene before an employee became a turnover risk.

Supervisors Make "Rounds," Too— Performance Conversations in a Hospital

Each day, doctors go about checking on their various patients in the hospital, also known as "making the rounds." A set of mid-Atlantic hospitals instituted a variation on performance conversation meetings with all their staff to address employee turnover and engagement. A good economy allows one's competitors to poach staff members in the competition for talent. It is wise to stay ahead of the competition and have frequent conversations with staff to head off any disengagement, concerns, or lethargy.

An audiologist might be tempted if a competitor called to offer an advancement opportunity. Many night nurses would jump at a recruiter's presentation of better shifts during a nursing shortage. Housekeeping staff might also be poached for a small wage increase. How would a manager know if an employee is considering an advancement, is tired of working nights, or has financial challenges at home? The answer is obvious—she would not know unless she were communicating with her employees. Regular communication is good, but open and honest communication is the best. Managers making their "rounds" every month made a noteworthy impact on turnover and increased employee engagement scores significantly. The solution to many organizational problems is the magic of communication between two people. Leaders can learn a lot by paying attention to employees and their needs. The Performance Improvement System and the Performance Conversations method work in any environment.

Performance Conversations, Questions, and Checklists

The Performance Conversations method can be deployed in different ways. First, the principles in the Performance Improvement System (feedback, feedforward, frequency, follow-up, and familiarity) must be utilized. Then, the foundational elements of the model must be incorporated. This includes brief, structured, planned, and periodic conversations; an improvement-focused partnership between the performer and coach; and the use of questions to stimulate and guide the dialogue. These elements work together to ensure success.

This book provides three applications of the method. The first is the Performance Portfolio technique, which uses evidence to drive dialogue and make good decisions; the second is the Performance Questions technique, a streamlined and focused version of the original method; and finally, the Performance Conversations Checklist, which broadens the scope and application of the model to handle the volume and complexities of various work environments. Table 4.2 provides a quick reference comparison of the three techniques.

Table 4.2. Performance Conversations Techniques: Similarities and Differences

	Performance Portfolio	Performance Questions	Performance Checklists
	Thirty-minute conversation	Thirty-minute conversation	Thirty-minute conversation
Primary tool	Performance logs	Seven Questions	Checklists
Question use	Sharing evidence and questions	Questions	Questions and prompts
Prior preparation	Required	Optional	Optional
Form/Instrument	Optional	Slate of questions	Checklist
Meeting summary	Required	Built-in	Optional
Evidence and artifacts	Required	Optional	As needed
Elements	Performance Log	N/A	N/A
	Performance Portfolio	N/A	N/A
	Annual summary	N/A	N/A

Swiss Army Knife of Performance Improvement

The Performance Conversations method could truly be the Swiss Army knife equivalent to performance improvement according to its design. The technique incorporates four reinforcing theories of working with people and five management principles, and its methods are built upon sound, proven practice.

Having provided scientific justification for the method, explained the principles that bring it to life, described the classic implementation (the Performance Portfolio), and highlighted some examples, it is now time to expand our understanding of the method's potential. The next chapters will detail how to apply the method in new and novel ways—Performance Questions and Performance Conversations Checklists.

THE PERFORMANCE QUESTIONS

5

Performance Questions:
The Magnificent Seven Questions

Judge a man by his questions rather than by his answers.
—Voltaire

The Magnificent Seven Questions comprise a carefully selected set of questions designed to achieve optimal performance outcomes. They are built upon years of research and professional practice and they represent the best intentions of most performance management systems. Using these seven questions will ensure that nearly every performance variable is tracked and managed. They provide a simple and elegant solution to managing and improving performance. There is no need for fancy forms and processes; long, confusing instruments; complicated routing systems; automated solutions; software installation; or flowcharts. Savvy managers and smart organizations can accomplish all their intended goals by following this intuitive outline.

The Performance Questions technique is a convenient way to employ the Performance Conversations method without the need for any special training or years of experience. As one gets more accustomed to the technique, he or she will be able to tailor the Magnificent Seven to their environment and work. One will eventually develop a unique set of questions optimal for each employee on one's staff.

The Magnificent Seven Questions are as follows:

1. What is going well?
2. What is not going well?
3. What else is going on?

4. What is the status of your goals, action plans, and follow-up items?
5. What can I do for you?
6. How are your professional relationships going?
7. How are you?

The phrasing and order of the Magnificent Seven Questions intentionally focus on the most important aspects of work. One may want to tailor the questions to one's voice after trying them in their original form. Nonetheless, be sure to keep to the intent of each question as outlined below.

What is going well? This question reinforces positive work outcomes. It uncovers or establishes what is good, why it is good, and how to keep it going. This question aims to acknowledge and celebrate successes, and take actions to replicate them.

What is not going well? This is the accountability and correction question. It discovers what is going wrong as soon as possible and seeks a solution. This is where the employee discloses problems and asks for help, or where the leader diagnoses the situation and determines the need for an intervention. The manager and employee decide the necessary adjustments and their implementation. Early disclosure or detection allows ample time for a course correction and redirection, change, or cessation of the unwanted performance.

What else is going on? This question is about sharing information. Every topic, no matter how big or small, can be discussed. General information can be insignificant, but it can also be insightful because it reveals patterns and trends before they would otherwise have been known. Seemingly mundane information can generate new ideas or suggestions for improvement. A healthy dose of stealth accountability is embedded within this question as well. It is hard for an employee to say they did not have an opportunity to inform the leader of relevant information earlier when a latent problem develops if this question is effectively utilized.

What is the status of your annual goals, action plans, and follow-up items? This is a classic management question with a focus on accomplishments, results, and efforts. It is a status report used to track and manage work. Whether goals are weekly, monthly, quarterly, or yearly, this is the occasion to have purview over their collective progress. This question can focus on the necessary continuity between short- and long-term work activities depending upon the length of time between check-ins. A performance conversation is different from day-to-day tasks and week-to-week meetings; they are concerned with the forest as the latter is concerned with individual trees.

What can I do for you? This is the single most important question a leader can ever ask an employee and should be asked often. The purpose of a manager is to help others accomplish work better than they would have been able to do alone. The outdated perspective that leaders get work done through other people implies that employees are not motivated and lack ownership or responsibility. Wise managers know that the key to success is helping others do their very best work. Good managers are coaches, enablers, supporters, and cheerleaders.

How are your professional relationships going? No one is an island and all work in an organization is completed through connection with others. This question aims to improve the linkages between people, functions, and the organization. We interact with people, we coordinate efforts with other functions, and we have a social contract with the organization. Each relationship matters. It is hard to perform our best when we do not like or get along with our coworkers, and work is inefficient and ineffective when departments or functions do not interface properly. When we do not feel like we belong within an organization, either our performance suffers, or we leave the organization.

How are you? This seemingly mundane and insignificant question is an undercover gold mine of performance. Many leaders mistakenly try to separate the performer from the person when in fact they are one in the same. Engagement is about discretionary effort. "If you do not know who I am or care about what I think and feel, I will never voluntarily give you 100% of my commitment and effort." Anything less is an exchange of time and labor for money, which does not engender full performance. This question recognizes that performance is a byproduct of a person, not just a performer.

Magnificent for Many Reasons

As noted, these questions provide an expert guide to achieving nearly all the objectives of most performance management systems with the added benefit of focusing on performance improvement, not performance documentation. Table 5.1 illustrates the typical purposes of performance management systems.

The Magnificent Seven Questions have universal appeal. They are the best available questions for most performance situations because they were custom-made to address the best intents of all performance management systems. The healthy mix of questions also gather, probe, and clarify information; encourage reflection; solve problems; stimulate ideas; and build rapport.

A careful analysis of these seven questions will reveal their depth, and understanding the meaning behind each one will reveal numerous truths. These questions encapsulate the best intentions of good supervision and performance management. The goal of each question is explained below, and complementary alternative and follow-up questions are provided in the chapters that follow.

Table 5.1. Typical Purposes of Performance Management Systems

Purposes	Performance Questions #
Accountability	1, 2, 3, 4
Administrative decisions (pay increases, promotions, layoffs, training eligibility, discipline, terminations)	All
Affirmation	1, 5, 7
Alignment (with team, department, or organizational goals, mission, strategies)	1, 2, 3, 4, 6
Career development	5, 7
Communication	All
Coordination	All
Documentation/Record keeping*	All**
Evaluation	1, 2, 3, 4
Feedback	1, 2, 3, 4, 5, 7
Goal management	All
Job duties/Description clarification/Update	1, 2, 3, 4
Performance improvement/Coaching	All
Performance management (supervision)	All

Purposes	Performance Questions #
Performance tracking	1, 2, 3, 4
Problem resolution	All
Promotion	1, 4, 5, 6, 7
Recognition and reward	1, 5, 7
Reflection	1, 2, 3, 4, 6
Relationship-building	3, 5, 7
Retention	5, 7
Skill development/Growth	2, 3, 5, 6, 7
Standards and expectations	1, 2, 3, 4
Training needs assessment	2, 3, 4, 5, 7

*When using the Performance Portfolio technique for documentation, the employee and manager are asked to keep and present performance logs and artifacts (reports, notes, letters, copies, photos, etc.) as evidence of the work performed.

** A summary of the Performance Questions meeting provides documentation for performance. Additionally, for legal purposes, it would be indefensible for an employee to claim they were not treated fairly if they had multiple opportunities to discuss and clarify work requirements; meet with their supervisor to talk about standards, expectations, and results; disclose problems or ask for help; and receive assistance from the supervisor. A general accountability is also established by having multiple performance conversations. Therefore, performance questions naturally provide a legal defense before a problem is ever presented.

Questions and Performance Conversations

The Performance Questions technique puts the Performance Conversations method into practice. It helps to keep the focus on the most important aspects of work by steering the conversation in the right direction. Preplanned questions ensure the conversation, attention, and effort stays on pertinent topics. Though the Magnificent Seven Questions are an ideal slate of questions, they are by no means the only way to approach this protocol. The alternative phrasing of asking about two things that one should stop, start, or continue doing is one example offered in Table 4.1. Organizations may develop their own ideal set of questions for their unique use.

Questions Are an Adaptable Management Technique

Questions are a simple and elegant way of addressing the intent of most performance management discussions. They provide an overview of the strategic, developmental, and administrative purposes of performance management, as well as the stated and unstated goals of feedback, accountability, and growth embedded in their practice.

Questions are useful because they can be easily modified, updated, and tailored to the specific setting and circumstances of an organization or for individual employees. The Performance Questions technique, an entirely new management system, uses a framework of five to nine questions as the basis of performance discussions. Uniquely, these questions can be modified by managers of different departments, locations, or levels within the organization according to the experience and performance record of individual employees, as well as the needs of the enterprise. The method produces a management tool of incredible flexibility and utility.

Every employee in the fictional ACME Corporation could be asked, "What is the status or your goals, action plans, and follow-up items that were required from our last performance conversation?" Vice presidents would respond on the status of strategic initiatives, business plans for each division, and the hiring process for the new director. Meanwhile, a director would report not only on the progress of operational changes and their efficacy, but also the status of personnel actions they have undertaken. An accountant might respond by saying she has not started on one of her annual goals, she is ahead of schedule on closing out the quarter's reconciliation statements, and she has registered for the conference approved for her professional development plan since the last conversation with her director. A computer analyst might report that a technology system upgrade has delayed him from meeting his goals and that he needs help prioritizing the remaining activities. This one question can be asked many ways and in many different settings with equally effective results.

Questions can be tailored to specific circumstances as long as the spirit and intent of the question are preserved. The question "What is the status or your goals, action plans, and follow-up items?" could be modified for a new employee and stated as "Do you understand how your annual goals, quarterly action plans, and follow-up items are interrelated? If so, let's talk about your progress. If not, let's talk about how to get there." For a veteran employee, it could be asked as simply as "Doug, are we hitting all of our targets?" or "Did you complete the list we created last month?" For an employee who does not have a history of stellar performance, the question or inquiry might be phrased as follows: "Could you share with me evidence of the successful completion of your assigned three projects?" or "Tell me what percentage complete you are on your long-term goals and if there are any outstanding items we need to talk about."

Strategic Use of Questions

A progressive company might ask every employee one key question each year, such as what one is doing to achieve a specific company goal. Important questions could be asked several times a year and at each performance conversation. A good example would be to ask each employee for one idea that would improve the company's operations or reduce costs. Suggestions for new product ideas or referrals of new customers or employees could also be solicited, depending upon the nature of the business. Performance Conversations can be used to align all employee efforts to achieve specific strategic objectives.

A Technique That Supports the Manager and the Employee

Every employee should be asked to prepare questions for their supervisor to ensure they are performing well and meeting expectations. Employees might ask, "In what three areas should I make a change now to ensure that I perform well later this year?" The Performance Questions technique has the unique ability to manage performance in a variety of helpful ways. With interactive dialogue, healthy conversations, communication, and cooperation, the focus stays on employee involvement, engagement, and improvement.

6

What Is Going Well?

A prudent question is one-half of wisdom.

—Francis Bacon

The Goal: Replicating Good Performance

"What is going well?" is a question that aims to make success transparent and routine. It is about clarity, acknowledgment, and reinforcement because replicating good performance requires conscious effort. We must know how to do our jobs well, why it creates success, and why it is important. This and related follow-up questions are about reproducing quality outcomes. In layman's terms, this question ensures that everyone knows what good performance looks like, what it is made of, and how it can be reproduced.

The purpose of this question is to produce results. Everyone is focused on the indicators and levels of quality when they are discussed. This makes all the difference for the purpose of increasing revenue, improving quality, lowering costs, earning new customers, or other organizational goals. Asking questions about what is going well should draw out information and cause the employee to reflect upon their work. The goal is to acknowledge and replicate the actions and activities that the employee is doing right. The poker metaphor most applicable here is that we intentionally double down on our successes.

A Recognition Tool

"What is going well?" is also a great way to start a conversation because it is positive. It is oriented toward the future, which keeps attention on things that can be affected as opposed to things from the past that cannot be changed. This question also gives the supervisor a natural prompt and opportunity to recognize and praise good performance. It is an upbeat segue into sharing information that will help the employee relax and settle into the conversation. It will also allow the manager to build rapport with the employee before covering more difficult topics. Ideally, this question will become pro forma in that there should always be positive performance indicators to discuss during the conversation.

A Focus on the Most Important and Highest Priority Items

It is important to ensure that the employee is working on the most important priorities when asked the question "What is going well?" A status report on items of secondary importance is less desirable. If an employee is not reporting on outcomes and successes in the major areas of their work or items of highest priority, then their attention and effort should be redirected. A more pointed question like "Are things going well with X, Y, and Z?" may be better suited for quality assurance in certain circumstances. A lackluster or vague response to this question is a sign of concern.

Follow-Up Questions Are a Good Follow-Up Technique

> *Follow-up questioning is a normal part of conversation,*
> *and probing strategies should be considered an extension*
> *of that approach. For mistakes in reasoning, analysis,*
> *or by omission, good follow-up questions can bring out*
> *the cogent details in the normal course of questioning.*
> —Terry Fadem[32]

Just as Follow-up is a part of the Fabulous Five Performance Improvement System, follow-up questions are also necessary ingredients to a good conversation. Our Magnificent Seven Questions are complemented by alternative and follow-up questions to produce a solid repertoire of inquiry tools. An alternative way of asking "What is going well?" is "What is going according to plan?" We must know what creates success and how it can be recreated because good performance is an intentional act, not luck or happenstance. Follow-up questions clarify, focus, or redirect questions and information; they gather related data; and continue certain lines of inquiry. "How do we get this same level of achievement each time?" is invaluable to closing the loop from establishing expectations to making sure success is attained and repeated.

Alternative Questions

- Are things going well with X, Y, and Z?
- What is going well and according to our plan?
- What is going as well as you had expected?
- What evidence do we have to show that things are going well?
- What has occurred in the past few weeks of which you are most proud?
- Are things working well normally?
- What are the top three things going well lately?
- Do you have two or three examples of things that are going well?
- What are the activities that have become routine or on autopilot?
- How do you know you are doing a good job?
- Have you received any compliments lately?

Follow-Up Questions

- How do we get this same level of success each time?
- What can we do to ensure this same level of quality every time?
- Do you expect any changes that could keep you from repeating this good work?
- What did you specifically do to make things turn out so well?
- Do you need any assistance or resources to help you keep up the good work?
- Are these positive outcomes a result of the system's design?
- Are these positive outcomes a result of your training?
- What can we learn from our successes?
- How could we take things to the next level?

7

What Is Not Going Well?

If you do not know how to ask the right
question, you discover nothing.

—W. Edwards Deming

The Goal: Adjusting and Correcting

The question "What is not going well?" is about accountability. However, it is a positive question if it is asked early, correctly, and with the right intent in a spirit of partnership. It can improve productivity if it is meant to uncover challenges, obstacles, and mistakes so that the supervisor and employee can determine future actions together. It is counterproductive if it is asked to rate someone's performance, lay blame, or hold someone solely accountable for a mistake. This question has the potential to be the difference between success and failure when the employee knows he or she is being given the opportunity to ask for help by a supportive supervisor who will help find a solution while there is still time for change.

The supervisor must intend to help earnestly because if they do not, the supervisor risks the employee holding back important or damaging information. Some employees might even try to hide negative information in the hopes that it will not be discovered. A positive relationship with an employee is important to ensuring this question receives honest answers. Proper use of this question will uncover information and obstacles, and troubleshoot problems. In simpler terms, it is about finding and removing barriers impeding success.

The beauty of this question is that it gently presents accountability. Employees know that they will be asked the question "What is not going well?" multiple times. Failing to divulge what is not going well when asked clearly and directly could be perceived as being dishonest, neglectful, or even incompetent. It is usually easier and less painful to disclose pertinent information at the earliest opportunity. Once mentioned, it can be dealt with. A wise saying reminds us that "bad news does not get better with age." Hiding problematic information can be perceived to be an intentionally destructive act, not a mere oversight. Waiting to mention, or concealing situations that are not going well when asked multiple times, is likely enough grounds for disciplinary action and possibly termination.

Opportunity for Intervention and Help

Asking "What is not going well?" creates the opportunity for a manager to intervene and act, as well as work with the employee to make necessary corrections and adjustments to performance. The manager might provide tools, training, support, encouragement, help, or other resources, as necessary. An employee will find it comforting to know they will be given multiple opportunities to ask for assistance and support to get to the finish line on time. If delivered correctly and with good intention, few employees would not see the value in fully answering this question.

Coach Me, Please!

Accountability is not a bad word when it is used during an improvement process and not as a measurement stick. Most people want to do a good job, and they will if given the right tools, methods, environment, and (most importantly) guidance and support. In other words, they need the right supervisor. Great managers know how to ask the right questions, including "What is preventing you from producing A+ work?" or "What problems have you encountered lately?" They know that the role and purpose of a supervisor is to create the environment and opportunity for others to do their very best work. This requires some heavy lifting, mainly finding and solving problems. Many of us would be unemployed if all employees could and would do excellent work without a supervisor. Just as every great athlete has a great coach, every employee deserves a stellar manager who is eager and able to support them by helping to address problems, challenges, and mistakes.

Alternative Questions

- What is preventing you from producing A+ work?
- What problems have you encountered recently?
- What obstacles have prevented you from meeting your objectives/deadlines/targets?
- What are the indicators of things not going well?
- What workplace concerns do you have?
- What problems or issues have you had recently with coworkers, customers, equipment, tools, or resources that have affected your work?
- What have been the last three work assignments that you have had trouble completing?
- Do you have any personal issues that affect your work performance?
- What information have you not shared that might be useful for us to discuss?
- What information are you reluctant or afraid to share because you are concerned about my reaction?
- How could your work be completed differently?

Follow-Up Questions

- What is the plan to get things correctly working again?
- What results should we expect from our planned actions?
- What happened next?
- Why do you think these things happened?
- Why do you think this is a potential concern?
- What could be the possible cause of these occurrences?
- What do you specifically need help with to ensure you produce A+ work next time?
- What can or will you do differently after this conversation?
- What is preventing you from doing things the right way?
- Who else was involved in these challenges?
- Who should be involved in getting things back on track?
- Why?
- What can we learn from our challenges (mistakes)?
- Do you have suggestions about how we might…?
- How did the problem(s) occur?

- Why did they occur?
- Who else shares some responsibility in making this successful?
- Are there equipment, system, process, or resource problems that contribute to these challenges?
- What can be done to ensure these challenges do not reoccur?
- Is there someone else who might be able to help you do this better?
- Is there someone else who might be better able to do this work?
- What can I help you with?
- How will we know when we are being successful?
- What do we know and what do we not know about this situation?
- What have we learned from this situation?
- Why choose to do X instead of Y?
- Are we dealing with symptoms or the real problem?
- What are the signs or symptoms of how things are going?
- What information or facts should we investigate to fully address what is going on here?
- Why do we do it this way?
- What work should we stop doing?
- In what ways can this be improved?
- What is keeping you from doing the things you know are most important?

What Else Is Going On?

*A wise man can learn more from a foolish question
than a fool can learn from a wise answer.*

—Bruce Lee

The Goal: Identifying Opportunities for Improvement or Problem Prevention

"What else is going on?" is a neutral question designed to stimulate conversation and information sharing. It is impossible to predict the number of responses to this question, which is precisely why it is invaluable. Its open-ended nature gathers information regarding the work, work environment, or employee that may prove useful now or in the future. It is complementary to "What is going well?" and "What is not going well?" because it addresses those situations in the gray area that cannot be anticipated, preplanned, or possibly even known by the supervisor. Oftentimes, future successes are discussed, and potential problems are prevented in response to this performance question. It is an information sharing, discovery, and future possibilities question.

Every topic, no matter how big or small, can be discussed, whether it is directly or indirectly related to work, a byline, a curiosity, or a "nice-to-know." This question serves as a communication channel so that everyone is kept up to date. Ideas can be generated in the work banter, ways to improve current practices can be discussed, misunderstandings can be reasoned, and quality indicators can be clarified. This question can be used as an early alert of situations or methods that may become important in the future. Employees might also use this time to bring up personal issues that affect them or their work. Finally, this question is an opportunity for a manager to learn information that would have otherwise stayed unknown if such a general, open-ended question had not been asked. While seemingly trivial, "What else is going on?" is a powerful question with dozens of potential uses.

Stealth Accountability

A healthy dose of stealth accountability is embedded within this question as well. It would be difficult for an employee to say they did not have the opportunity to inform the supervisor of a potentially important piece of information if they had undergone several Performance Conversations and been asked this question. It also encourages the employee to stay involved and engaged in the discussion, as this is their opportunity to determine the topic of conversation. One caution is that it can quickly deteriorate into a conversation about the weather, grandkids, or new guy in Accounting. "What else is going on?" is about the things that affect work. Managers should therefore steer the conversation in the direction of high work priorities. Alternate phrasings, follow-up questions, or statements can be used, such as "What else is going on with your work/at work/in general?"

Neutral information is often the source of the next challenge or opportunity. This question provides the open-ended space for status reports, general performance indicators, or early alerts of things that may become important later. Alternative questions include "What question should I be asking that I have not asked?" and "What did you think about sharing that you did not share yet?" The "What else is going on?" question can also be structured in a more strategic fashion by including specific topics related to an individual's work. This could be a project, report, status of interpersonal relationships with coworkers, follow-up plan, specific area of one's job description, professional development plan, or nearly anything else work-related. Some examples are "What is up with the Thompson Report and your other work?" "What is going on with the disagreement we had with Accounting over last quarter's billing?" and "What else has been happening in the department that I might not know about?"

Alternative Questions
- Are there any interesting things going on lately?
- What should be the focus of our conversation today?

- What is on your mind?
- What else is going on with your work, at work, or generally?
- What else should I know that I have not asked about already?
- What else should we talk about that we have not talked about already?
- What are people talking about?
- What are the major indicators or examples of work that we should talk about?
- What information or indicators should we be tracking to describe the work we are doing?
- Is there anything you want to tell me or that I should know?
- What else has been happening that I might not know about?
- What topic did we forget to talk about?
- What information did you think about sharing before this meeting that you did not share yet?
- Do you feel like we are on the right path?

Follow-Up Questions
- What does all this mean to us here at work?
- Can we use this information to make work better?
- Why did you think that was an important topic to share with me?
- With whom should we share this information?
- Is there anything you want to know about?
- Is there anything you want to learn about?
- What information should I know now that might end up being a problem later if I remain uninformed?
- Is there anything that you were planning to share at some point in the future that you can share now?
- Have you had any good ideas about work lately?
- What are our alternatives?
- Are you satisfied with how things are going?
- What keeps you up at night, or what are you most worried about at work?
- What is your biggest, seemingly unconquerable challenge whose resolution would make your work experience better?
- What are you afraid of happening at work?

What Is the Status of Your Goals, Action Plans, and Follow-Up Items?

*Listening is the front end of decision making.
It's the surest, most efficient route to informing
the judgments you will need to make.*

—Bernard T. Ferrari[33]

The Goal: Determining Next Steps

"What is the status of your goals?" is a classic management question that asks for a progress report on work activities. It tracks and manages efforts, outcomes, and behaviors to verify they are aligned with established objectives within the set time period. Whether goals are daily, weekly, monthly, quarterly, or yearly, checking in is how managers maintain purview over work activities. Responses to this question and its alternatives inform managers about the progress being made (or lack thereof) and help them determine next steps.

Coaching in Action

Out of the Magnificent Seven, this question is where managers can best serve as a coach. Regardless of the employee's response, the manager must decide and act. This can be offering praise for a job well-done, giving a pep talk for things that are lagging, giving a "kick in the butt" for things that are behind, or making corrections for things that are offtrack. If all is well, the manager focuses on other priorities. Not all goals are formal or laid out in the same framework and language, so this question has three parts to account for both informal and formal activities. Whether it is daily, monthly, or project work, many things must be accomplished in any workplace. Using the framework of goals can facilitate the tracking of routine, project, and long-term work.

Goal-Oriented

The best approach to this question includes agreeing upon goals in advance, identifying interim milestones, and establishing the measures by which goals will be evaluated. Goal achievement is facilitated by identifying targets, metrics, and measures as indicators of progress. Ideally, long-term goals are divided into smaller time frames and metrics are specified for each interval. This allows managers to intervene early and adjust if necessary at the first sign that things are offtrack. Many have found it useful to have long-term goals dependent on short-term action plans. Others use colors to provide a quick status on goal progress, with green indicating things are progressing as planned, yellow meaning things are progressing slower than expected, and red indicating things are not going well or are offtrack completely. Automated goal management software is also common these days.

Another smart technique is to add a strategic element to each employee's goals. Organizational goals are assigned to operational units and then broken down further to departments, teams, and individuals. Cascading goals to employees form the building blocks of performance and are tracked by managers in their regular performance conversations with staff members. This deliberate effort to connect individuals, coworkers, teams, departments, and divisions is good management practice. Regular progress reports allow a manager to check these links and ensure their strength.

The Big Picture of Goals and Plans

Asking "What is the status of your goals?" during a feedback session is different than asking about day-to-day work. It is not a conversation about what tasks must be completed to achieve a specific project, task, or goal. Instead, it is an opportunity to look at the big picture and patterns, not individual actions.

While the objective of this question is to gather information to determine how to intervene, there may be a temptation to jump in and solve problems uncovered on the spot. This is not the purpose of a performance conversation. The purpose of a thirty-minute, one-on-one feedback session using the Performance Conversations approach is to holistically examine how things are connected and how they work or do not work well together. It is stepping back to make meaning out of the trends, and informal and formal tendencies that emerge to silently affect how things work overall. Uncorrected habits become standard protocol if left unchecked. It ensures that the correct work is being performed, the right resources are being utilized, and everyone knows their role in creating success.

Its perspective implies questions such as:

- Are we managing the right goals?
- Do these goals accomplish departmental and organizational objectives?
- If these goals are not accomplished, what will be the larger impact on the company?
- Should we notify other departments or upper management that we have encountered unanticipated obstacles when working on this goal?
- Are these goals still relevant given recent changes?

When an issue is uncovered, the manager should acknowledge it and schedule a time to address it with the employee. Otherwise, the performance conversation may devolve into a tactical discussion about one specific operational matter, instead of a heady discussion about larger matters of more importance.

Goal Management and Quality Assurance

"What is the status of your goals?" is a high-level review of collective progress that makes sure objectives are communicated and coordinated across people, time, and organizations. Asking it is a practice that ensures work, as a whole, is completed on time, within budget, and in accordance with agreed upon plans.

> *When you ask for people's opinions and take them seriously,*
> *you are sending a powerful message: "You have great*
> *ideas. I believe in you. You can do this." Just asking can*
> *empower people to do things they couldn't do on their own.*
> —Tony Stoltzfus[34]

A valuable tip about encouraging employee engagement is sharing responsibility with the employee and asking, "What is the status of *our* goals?" This helps build rapport and partnership with the employee. Employees feel empowered when they know they are not performing alone, but instead have a good coach standing by who is as engaged in their success as they are. Other alternative questions include "How are you tracking your goals?," "Are we tracking your goals the right way?," and "Which activities in your action plans have you completed recently?" A goal will not be accomplished if it is not tracked or if the employee cannot provide an affirmative response regarding their project status.

Alternative Questions
- What is the status of our goals?
- Are you on track to achieve agreed upon goals?
- Are we tracking your goals the right way?
- How do you know if a goal is off track?
- Which activities in your action plans have you completed recently?
- Which interim results have you achieved related to your goals?
- What are the pieces of evidence or indicators that results are on track?
- Are the goals we agreed upon progressing as planned?
- On which of your goals are you ahead of schedule, and which of them are you behind schedule?
- For which of your goals have you not yet met target dates?
- For which of your goals is achievement unrealistic at this point?
- Do you need any help achieving any of the goals for this year?
- Which of the goals that we are tracking are most important at this time?
- Should we shift our time, attention, or resources toward one or more of our plans or actions at this time?
- Do we have all the resources necessary to achieve each of our goals and plans?
- Which activities should we celebrate as interim successes?

Follow-Up Questions
- What evidence do you have that can demonstrate all your goals are on track?

- Have you completed your thirty- and ninety-day action plans?
- What does your status report on goals and plans really mean?
- If we complete everything we have planned, will that ensure we are successful with everything we need to do?
- Are we tracking the right goals?
- Does our tracking and reporting system give us the right information about what is going on?
- Are the things we are tracking really important?
- What are the things we should track instead of the things we are tracking?
- Are the goals we created last _____ still relevant?
- What will happen if we do not complete these goals the way we planned?
- What are your plans for your work over the coming days/weeks/months?

What Can I Do for You?

Given that questions drive thoughts, feelings, and actions, they undoubtedly drive results as well.

—Marilee Adams[35]

The Goal: Coaching and Removing Obstacles

"What can I do for you?" is the single most important question a manager can ever ask an employee and should be asked as often as possible. It sends all the right messages and can practically be a complete Performance Conversations session in and of itself. It makes the employee feel empowered to act and entrusted to know what needs to be done. However, they know they still have help if necessary. The purpose of a manager is to help others accomplish work better than they would working alone. This is in contrast to the outdated perspective that managers get work done through others. The former unleashes employee potential; the latter implies a lack of motivation, ownership, and responsibility.

No Excuses

Wise managers know that the key to success is helping others do their very best work—aka, to coach them to success. They must provide employees with guidance, direction, training, support, and encouragement. "What can I do for you?" is a masterful coaching question that creates a healthy environment for feedback and information exchange. Most importantly, it removes obstacles and excuses. The employee can never truly provide a good reason for why they did not accomplish a task or goal. This question is a healthy way to make employees ultimately responsible for their outcomes. It says, while you are responsible and there are no excuses, you are not expected to do it alone.

A 21st-Century Classic

"What can I do for you?" should become a classic 21st-century management question as it reflects the reality of supervising knowledge workers. Today's employees have unique knowledge, talents, and skills. The manager is not a know-it-all and can never do it all. A performance partnership is formed when the coach on the sideline empowers and enables the athlete on the field to perform at a higher level. This is the role and relationship that the manager and employee should have with one another. Therefore, in a sense, the manager works for the employee and embodies the tenants of servant leadership. If the manager does not create a multiplicative effect on the employee's performance outcomes, then the manager represents nothing more than unnecessary overhead costs.

The Manager Is Much Obliged

Another way of asking this question is "What can I do for you to help you do your very best work?" When repeated over a long period, it helps build trust and confidence between the coach and performer and the partnership grows. Embedded here also is an appropriate amount of accountability, support, and quality assurance since both parties are co-performers and have a shared responsibility for outcomes. They both become committed to the employee's success, and the manager becomes obliged to provide the right resources, tools, guidance, assistance, and support. There is no excuse for an employee's failure.

The Courage to Change

However, adopting this servant leader perspective may require a bit of courage. Managers may not like the answer they receive when they ask this question. What if the employee discloses that her manager's supervision is not helpful, that their relationship is counterproductive, or that her interactions with the manager are not as positive as the interactions she sees the manager have with other employees? While the answers to "What can I do for you?" might be sobering, they should be welcomed because they will help the manager and employee make the necessary changes to produce optimal performance.

Alternative ways of asking this question include "What do you need to continue to perform well?" and "How can I best support you?" Good follow-up questions are "Is there anything else you need to achieve your goals?" and "What would be one change that could help you work better?"

Alternative Questions

- What can I do to help you do your very best work?
- What do you need to continue to perform well?
- How can I best support you?
- What do you need from others to help you perform?
- What is inhibiting and what is helping your performance?
- Do you get too little, too much, or the right amount of feedback?
- Do you get too little, too much, or the right amount of support?
- Each employee and manager have a certain work style. What do I do that helps you perform your best?
- What can I do to make your work life easier?
- What could we do to make your job more exciting, interesting, or challenging?

Follow-Up Questions

- If we make the changes we discussed, will this guarantee you will produce A+ work?
- If we looked back next year and reflected on why we were not successful, what would be potential reasons?
- Is there anything else you need to achieve your goals?
- Do you have all the resources, tools, or equipment necessary for your success?
- Are there any obstacles that prevent you from performing at your best every day?
- What would be one change that could help you work better?
- What are two things that I do as a manager that help you the most and least?
- Do you get enough, too much, or the right amount of my attention?

- Give me examples of when I have given you too little or too much autonomy.
- How does my supervisory style help or inhibit how you work?
- How would you describe me as a supervisor?
- What questions do you have for me?
- Are there questions about the organization, department, team, or job that I can answer for you?
- Do you know my expectations?
- What are your expectations of me as a supervisor?
- If you could ask the CEO one question, what would it be?
- If there were one more thing that you would like to accomplish at work this year, what would it be?

11

How Are Your Professional Relationships Going?

You've got to ask! Asking is, in my opinion, the world's most powerful—and neglected—secret to success and happiness.
—Percy Ross

The Goal: Coordination, Integration, Relationships, and Retention

Asking "How are your professional relationships going?" improves the bonds between people and their functions and organization. No one is an island and all work in an organization is completed with others. We interact with people, we coordinate efforts with other departments, and we have a social contract with the organization. Each of these relationships matter! It is hard to perform our best when we do not like or get along with coworkers, and work is inefficient and ineffective when departments and functions clash with one another. When we believe in the company's mission, vision, products, and goals, we have an emotional connection that breeds loyalty, commitment, and passion for our role. When we do not feel like we belong within an organization, performance suffers.

Interpersonal relationships color our private, personal, and professional lives. Experts agree that a major difference between a group of people and a team is the synergy that develops from strong emotional and social connections between participants. Good teams are made up of people who want to perform well not just for themselves, but for each another. "How are your professional relationships going?" is a maintenance check to make sure that things are okay between the employee and their peers, coworkers, customers, vendors, and work network.

Two of the most important aspects of production in an organization are the coordination and support between departments and knowing how one's work affects the timing, quality, and efficiency of others' jobs. Organizations are designed to work together—Marketing supports Sales, Accounting supports Finance, and Human Resources supports every department. It is imperative to give attention to, and take deliberate action to manage and maintain the interrelationships between departments and functions. Communication, coordination, and cooperation form the basis of an effective liaison.

Do I Matter?

According to employee engagement experts, an organization's mission, vision, strategy, and work are optimized when employees know why their role matters and how it connects to the bigger picture. Engagement is the discretionary effort put forth when work has more meaning than just completing tasks. What an employee feels about how and where they work matters a great deal. "How are your professional relationships going?" creates the opportunity for the manager to learn how an employee feels about what they are doing and with whom they are working. It is also a great time to reaffirm the employee and tell them why their role matters and how they connect with and improve the work of others.

Employees will leave if they feel disconnected, isolated, or that they do not belong. Therefore, asking questions is a turnover prevention tool. Managers get an advance warning of concerns and can intervene to prevent the employee's relationship with others from taking a downward spiral. Gallup has a now famous survey of employee engagement that has been administered millions of times over decades, and rightfully so. It is truly able to measure an employee's sense of connection with an organization. Significantly, two of the twelve questions ask, "Do you have a best friend at work?" and "Does your supervisor, or someone at work, seem to care about you as a person?"

Relationships, Connections, and Linkages

The question "How are your professional relationships going?" is about connection, linkage, integration, belonging, and purpose. Additional ways of asking this question include "Do you know how your work is connected with others?" and "Do you feel connected to the mission of the company and its products?" The heart of this question is monitoring the network of interactions between people, things, ideas, and, of course, the organization. Loose connections will likely produce lackluster performance and retention challenges. The "Do you have a best friend at work?" Gallup survey question tests the strength of the links and emotional bonds between the employee and those that surround him or her. There are other questions that can gauge the employee's thoughts and feelings about the organization as well. These include "Do you use the products and services that we sell?", "Do you have any challenges or issues with other departments?", "What bugs you the most about working here?", and "What do you like most about working here?" Asking questions like these is a good way to identify the bonds between employees, others, and the organization.

Alternative Questions

- Do you know how your work is connected with others?
- How are you doing with your peers and colleagues?
- How is the relationship with other departments or functions?
- Does your professional network assist you in the work you do every day?
- How do we know that your professional relationships are strong?
- Are you aware of how your work affects others?
- How is your work connected to other people, places, and functions within the organization?
- Do you know how what you do every day connects with the organization's strategy, the department's plans, and your team's goals?
- What are some good examples that show you are fitting in well?
- Do you feel like you are part of what makes this company great?
- Do you feel valued here?
- Do you think that everyone here is valued regardless of his or her race, gender, national origin, or other demographic?
- Would you recommend this organization to your family and friends as a good place to work?

Follow-Up Questions

- Are you getting along with everyone?
- Do you have friends at work?
- Is there anyone at work with whom you have problems working?

- Do you know why what you do is important?
- Do you know how or why what you do matters?
- Do you feel connected to the mission of the company and its products?
- Do you use the products and services that we sell?
- Are our vendor relationships helpful?
- Do you have any challenges or issues with other departments?
- What bugs you the most about working here?
- What do you like the most about working here?
- Do you have any coworkers that you think deserve recognition for their work?
- Which of your coworkers do you rely on most?

12

How Are You?

Questions provide the key to unlocking
our unlimited potential.

—Tony Robbins

The Goal: Removing Obstacles and Growing Rapport, Relationships, and Retention

"How are you?" might seem like a mundane question, but really it is a gold mine of performance in hiding. Many managers mistakenly try to separate the performer from the person, when in reality, they are two sides of the same coin. Employee engagement is about discretionary effort. As noted earlier, a silent cry of employees everywhere could be "If you do not know who I am, or care about what I think and feel, I will never voluntarily give you 100% of my loyalty and effort." Anything less than full commitment is an exchange of time and effort for dollars. This question recognizes that performance is a byproduct of a person, not a performer. Everyone wants to feel like they matter, and everyone wants to be viewed as a singular, unique individual. This basic human desire is as old as Aristotle's wisdom on the subject.

One might ask why the question "How are you?" is asked last rather than first. The reason is simple; this comes from learned experience. If the answer is too heavy, emotional, negative, or personal in a way that overshadows work (e.g. I am getting a divorce, I am pregnant, I am still grieving the loss of my favorite cousin, I think I am depressed, etc.), the response can make work seem irrelevant. If it is lighthearted, fun, funny, or interesting to both parties (e.g. I'm getting married, I'm buying a house, I really love working here, I just bought one of our products, etc.), it gives the two permission to go on a tangent that might consume too much time. When asked at the end, the conversation is limited to the available time or the two can agree to keep the conversation going if they have the luxury to do so.

It Is Not Personal...or Is It?

"How are you?" cultivates a personal relationship with employees necessary for optimal performance. A supervisor should be a coach, and the most effective coaches intimately know the performer's personality, behavior, habits, preferences, style, and other characteristics unique to who they are as an individual. This insight is used to help the performer succeed. While many may challenge the notion that a supervisor and employee should have a personal relationship of any type to any degree, doing so ignores the obvious. Everyone would agree that they performed their best at the hands of a childhood ballet teacher, Little League coach, math teacher, or former boss who took an interest in them as a person. These mentors wanted us to achieve our highest potential because they knew that if we were better personally and mentally, we would perform better athletically, academically, or professionally. This is the essence of good coaching.

Genuinely asking someone how they are doing and actually caring about their response will mean a lot to them—guaranteed. Do not bother asking the question if it is in a neutral but polite manner, like coworkers asking, "How are you today?" robotically each morning. It is insulting when someone only pretends to care about you and your response.

This Is Too Personal

The risk in asking this question is the conversation could go on a tangent into things that are not important, work-related, relevant, or appropriate. It is the manager's responsibility to keep the conversation on track. Learning about husbands, wives, kids, grandkids, hobbies, vacations, or even the weather is acceptable as some of this will undoubtedly be meaningful at one time or another to what is happening at work. An employee may take vacation every year during their child's spring break, leave early on their wedding anniversary, or pursue the next raise because they have kids entering college. Even knowing an employee's favorite color will matter if you ever buy them a gift. These are all examples of why knowing some personal information is necessary for a good working relationship. Clearly, financial challenges, marital problems, misbehaving kids, or drunken escapades during the last vacation are off-limits and should be discouraged when conversing with an employee.

The Person behind the Performance

The primary reason to ask, "How are you?" is to see how the employee is doing in regard to their work environment. This intent can be easily lost. The answer to this confusion is found by asking in the right context. A manager can ask an employee what is going on at work during a meeting if for no other reason than to make sure no personal or professional issues will have a negative impact on their work. Missing the fact that an employee is still grieving a year after losing a parent, ignoring a failing employee's cry for encouragement, or forgetting an employee's birthday will likely cause a downward spiral in performance. We must remember that an employee performing work is also an individual subject to feelings, emotions, thoughts, and other human frailties. We must nurture the person and the performer to cultivate success.

"How Are You?" (at Work)

"How are you?" can be pointedly phrased to lessen the risk of the conversation devolving into trivial discussions about non-work-related matters. Questions like "Do you feel good about the work you're doing?", "Are you doing okay here at work?", and "Is there anything affecting your work that I don't know about?" keep the focus on the workplace. The balance is cultivating enough information to be knowledgeable of the employee, but not so much as to make conversations too chummy. Follow-up questions provide both tactical and tactful ways of keeping the conversation civil, pleasant, personal, and professional. Two good follow-up questions that can redirect conversations toward the workplace are "Is your work still challenging and satisfying?" and "Is everyone treating you fairly at work?"

Alternative Questions
- Are you doing okay here at work?
- Is there anything negatively affecting your work that I do not know about?

- What are some good examples of things going well for you at work?
- Is your work-life balance manageable?
- Does anything concern you about work?
- Do you know people at work who value you and enjoy working with you?
- Is there anything at work you would like to do that you do not get a chance to do?
- What pleases you the most about _____ (organization, department, role, etc.)?
- Are you doing okay these days?
- Are things going well for you at work?
- Is there anything keeping you from being your best?
- What is on your mind these days about work?
- Is there anything work-related keeping you up at night?
- Are you learning everything you want to learn?
- Are you still growing at work?
- What are you most passionate about in life?
- What do you wish you could spend more time doing?
- Do you know everything that you think you need to know?
- What is one of the best days that you have had at work over the past year?

Follow-Up Questions
- Is your work still challenging and satisfying?
- If you could change one thing at work, what would it be?
- Are you getting asked to do too much or too little work?
- Are people treating you fairly at home and at work?
- Do you have any hobbies or volunteer activities that are similar to the work you do here?
- Do you feel good about the work you are doing?
- Are you still okay with how things are going at work?
- Do you still feel good about the work that you do every day?
- Why did you choose this profession?
- What do you like most about your profession?
- What was your major in college?

- Has anything at work changed over recent months that concerns you?
- Is there anything else work-related that you would like to talk about?
- What have you learned lately?
- What surprises you the most about the things you have learned recently?

13

Did You Have a Question?

*It is better to know some of the questions
than all of the answers.*

—James Thurber

Questions Tailored to Your Work

What are the three to five most important aspects of one's business? What are the quality indicators that let one know whether these areas are going well and as planned? What are the variables that enhance or inhibit the opportunities for success in these areas? What can each employee do to contribute to their success? What tools, resources, or support can help each employee do their very best work?

Answering the questions above is over half of what it takes to develop a custom Performance Questions system. Simply refine these questions and put them into the structured Performance Conversations method framework. To undoubtedly create the best opportunity for maximizing each employee's potential, create questions that combine elements of the Magnificent Seven with the unique aspects of one's work. These questions will resonate with staff because they will be meaningful and reflect the work that employees accomplish every day. This stands in stark contrast to a dated, generic appraisal instrument designed by consultants and applied to all employees across departments, locations, and levels of work.

Employees can also be involved in question development. This wraps engagement, quality assurance, relevancy, and accountability into a nice, neat package. Employees will be able to aptly explain or justify their efforts, outcomes, and behaviors because they will have been involved in defining the factors, successes, and scales to which they will be held accountable later. Future performance discussions are made easier and impactful when employees are involved in the development of their performance questions.

The Best Questions

> *It's not the perfect questions that make the difference:*
> *you just need to help the person you are coaching*
> *think a little farther down the road than they*
> *will on their own. Trust the process to help the*
> *person, not the greatness of your insight.*
>
> —Tony Stoltzfus[36]

While the questions used to drive performance conversations are profoundly important, it is not vital for them to be perfect. They just need to initially approximate the most important aspects of work. The flexibility of questions also means they can be asked slightly differently each time and refined over conversations until one has the necessary prompt for desired responses. Over time, the manager and employee will simultaneously get better at formulating, asking, and responding to questions.

The best questions are those that work the best. Even if they are poorly worded, shakily delivered, or off-topic, they are good if the right information is exchanged in the ensuing conversation. Tony Stoltzfus's quote at the opening of this section speaks volumes. He explains that the asking of questions is more powerful than the questions themselves. The process of formulating and asking questions and staying actively engaged in open dialogue is more important than the actual words. The goal is advancing performance, so the best questions are those that help the manager and employee focus on the most important aspects of work and their improvement.

Nonetheless, to optimize the Performance Conversations experience, it is prudent to initially develop the best possible questions and then refine them over time. The opening paragraph of this chapter briefly explained the process that managers should go through to develop their primary Performance Conversations questions for staff:

1. Identify the three to five most important aspects of work.
2. Determine what performance indicators would describe the best possible outcomes.

3. Identify the key factors to creating success.
4. Develop a long list of questions that could determine whether successful outcomes are being produced or if they are evident.
5. Refine these questions.

A reasonable reaction to the steps above might be, "Is that it? This is too simple to work." It may be simple, but it is not easy to put in practice. The driving factors, key activities, or root causes that make the most difference are not always obvious. To apply the Pareto principle to the workplace, we spend 20% of our time doing activities with the biggest impact.

It will likely take some time, attention, and discipline to truly define the most important aspects of work and how they are affected by other activities. This will be easy if one currently has the luxury of spending most of their time on their most important priorities without distraction from unnecessary or annoying responsibilities. Otherwise, it might require some deep reflection to identify the core drivers, levers, and indicators of well-done work in one's department or business. However, once found, they will enrich conversations about work, goals, action, and improvement. This is what a good Performance Conversation is all about. It all starts from good questions built upon the right ideas.

We Are in This Together...Aren't We?

A word of advice offered from experience is to use the word "we" instead of "you" whenever possible. While this may sound like a feel-good, HR-speak way of talking to employees about work, it is just one of those little things that communicates a great deal. Asking an employee "What are you going to do to correct that problem?" communicates that he made a mistake and now he has to fix it, and it can come off as accusatory or blaming regardless of how skillfully one delivers the question. Instead, ask "What are we going to do to correct that problem?" It says that while there is an issue and the employee has to take corrective action, as the supervisor I am going to help you if necessary. Both questions hold the employee accountable for a mistake and its solution, nonetheless, using "we" has some distinct advantages. The question is less threatening, defines the relationship as supportive, and conveys your confidence that the employee can resolve the situation—albeit with some help. The word "we" strikes the right manager-coach tone and keeps questions in the discussion positive, effectively avoiding the negative, "you-did-it-again" tone that is possible when using "you."

How Many Questions?

There is no prescribed number of questions. It is suggested that the number of questions directly correlate with the work pace and frequency of Performance Conversations, with the caveat that a thirty-minute discussion is the goal. Planning and preparation are necessary to ensure conversations are structured and focused on only the most important items and do not become a grab bag of miscellany. If there are many pressing issues that need to be addressed but conversations are only held quarterly, consider adding more questions. If the work is clear and stable, more dispersed conversations and fewer questions may be appropriate. The Magnificent Seven Questions provide a practical framework indicating that five to nine questions are enough for a robust half-hour conversation given that the employee is likely to have questions of their own as well.

Your Magnificent Seven Questions

> *You can tell whether a man is clever by his answers.*
> *You can tell whether a man is wise by his questions.*
> —Naguib Mahfouz

After first following the five-step process provided earlier and comparing and contrasting your custom questions with the Magnificent Seven offered in the Performance Questions technique, it is time to establish your final slate of questions. As noted, the infinite flexibility afforded by this technique allows one to refine questions over time. A carefully considered and meticulously designed set of seven questions will always suffice as a starting point. After using them in conversation, the infinite tweaking and refinement process can begin, and the questions can be codified into a working performance improvement instrument.

Develop Your Own Instrument

Follow the suggestions previously offered in this chapter to develop one's own performance improvement instrument. Here are several different approaches to creating an instrument for guiding conversation.

- The Magnificent Seven Questions
- The three essential Performance Conversation questions, see Table 4.1
- Brainstorming your favorite work questions
- Deciding what is topical for your organization
- Evaluating organization-specific priorities
- Determining a funky combination of questions
- Settling on "now" and "later" questions

Additionally, Appendix H provides a performance improvement instrument that utilizes the Magnificent Seven. Appendix I uses the three essential questions from the Magnificent Seven to guide a performance conversation. Appendices J to M provide four different examples of putting this concept into practice. Appendix J is an example of designing a Performance Questions instrument around key drivers for an individual work environment. Next, Appendix K focuses on goal accomplishment, problem resolution, and professional development. Appendix L, is applicable to a sales organization whose major priorities are sales, leads, and repeat business. The fourth and final option, Appendix M, supports the My Favorite Work Questions approach mentioned earlier and its focus is on organizations that have customer-centric work environments.

This great variety of options highlight the utility of the Performance Questions technique. With slight adjustments, instruments can be developed to manage various groups, topics, or any other appropriate business priority. The topical approach could be used to manage categories of work like goals, training, performance, behavior, recognition, customers, sales, costs, suggestions, or any other area of emphasis. Similarly, another approach that can be used in a department or across an organization, is to ensure everyone is focused on prescribed strategic performance variables such as innovation, sales, process improvement, or cost-savings. These could dovetail into strategic plans, annual goals, initiatives, HR strategies for individual and organizational performance, or any other factor deemed important by leaders.

Mixing and matching any of the ideas above to create unique sections of an instrument forms a funky combination that can make sense for an organization. A division could use two or three of the Magnificent Seven Questions in combination with three organization-specific questions, while also adding a separate section that tracks the employee's professional development and learning activities. This could be a clever approach for organizations with regulatory bodies that insist on tracking employees' continuing education hours. In the Performance Conversations approach, it is easy to adapt and allow one unit to amend the process to meet local objectives—all without the use of consultants or a time-consuming performance management system redesign. The activity is as simple as asking questions about unit-level priorities that matter a lot.

Infinite Variety and Flexibility in Instrument Design

There is an infinite variety of questions that can be asked; similarly, there is likely an infinite variety of ways to employ the Performance Questions technique. With this in mind, a company could plan to adjust their Performance Questions instrument each year or even each quarter to direct performance toward selected priorities. Automated performance management technology can make this extremely easy. In order to best drive performance, the instrument should be published at the beginning of the performance period so that everyone knows which variables are most important and employees can direct their time, effort, and attention in those directions.

What if the HR department publishes the following four questions in January?

1. What is your understanding of the company's new customer service initiative?
2. Do you know how your job contributes to delivering world-class customer service?
3. How would you rate your customer service efforts and that of your peers on a scale of 1–10? (Give examples to justify your response.)
4. Do you have any general company or specific department suggestions for improving customer service?

Imagine the hallway conversations, management meetings, individual initiatives, employee trainings, and activities that would be underway if everyone knew they would have to account for their time, effort, and attention at the end of March? The goal of the Performance Conversations method and Performance Questions technique is performance improvement, and such a focus would undoubtedly drive employee time, effort, and attention toward defined company priorities, such as in better customer service in the example above. If the CEO is pleased with the company's progress on that issue, the focus could be moved toward another organizational priority for the second quarter or next year. If not, the questions could be repeated or refined until the desired organizational end is achieved. The flexibility afforded by the Performance Questions technique provides a strategic and operational focus unlike any other performance management system.

On to the Next Question; But Wait, There Is More!

So, you have analyzed your work, created a good slate of questions or adopted the Magnificent Seven Questions, and created an instrument to prepare for or host performance discussions. What comes next? Now is the time to hold a thirty-minute conversation with staff about the most important aspects of their work. Chapter 16 is designed to provide advice on holding those conversations and keeping them focused, brief, and productive.

However, before going into the specifics of the half-hour conversation, there is an option to use another method. In addition to the Performance Questions and Performance Portfolio techniques is the Performance Conversations Checklist, offered next. Regardless of the method, questions are always used to drive the conversation and keep it focused on the highest work priorities. The Performance Conversations Checklist is easier to understand and practice after first discussing the Performance Portfolio and Performance Questions techniques as they offer the best examples of this new approach in action.

Performance Conversations Checklist Technique—Next

The checklist approach uses a list to track required elements that should be considered when holding conversations. The beauty of this method is that it tracks and monitors a variety of related topics over a period of time. For example, it is not necessary to discuss an employee's job description or career plans every six weeks, but the checklist ensures that they are discussed at least annually. Meanwhile, conversations about goals could be held quarterly. A checklist can help managers keep track of numerous topics and prompt them to act when needed.

IV

THE PERFORMANCE CONVERSATIONS CHECKLIST

14

Checklists: The Tool to Use for Important Matters

*...checklists seem able to defend anyone, even the experienced,
against failure in many more tasks than we realized. They
provide a kind of cognitive net. They catch mental flaws inherent
in all of us—flaws of memory and attention and thoroughness.
And because they do, they raise wide, unexpected possibilities.*

—Atul Gawande[37]

Checklists are used in many situations where lives are on the line because they are the ultimate quality-control, safety, and life-saving device. They are used as a management tool and preventative measure when the risk of forgetting points, missing details, or failing to apply proper procedures is so high that it might cause damage, death, or the loss of significant resources. A checklist is used by military officers, pilots, surgeons, and safety professionals when protocols really matter—a more useful tool for high-stakes professionals is almost inconceivable. While we do not need them to save lives, checklists can be used to preserve one's livelihood, business, or profits.

This is because checklists are expertise distilled down to the core elements. They reduce the wisdom of experience to linear kernels of knowledge accessible to everyone. Can checklists be considered ten years of experience in a box, a college degree in a paragraph, or wisdom in one's pocket? Maybe so! Checklists are truly a remarkable advance in management technology. It is a pity that the loss of life and limb is still prevalent today because people fail to use this simple, effective, and remarkable tool that has been around for thousands of years. We will use them here to manage performance, nonetheless.

Checklists Are a Cure for Ineptitude

Atul Gawande, author of the acclaimed book *The Checklist Manifesto*, argues that the complexity and velocity of change has made it increasingly easy for us to become inept.[38] In this context, ineptitude is defined as instances where appropriate knowledge is present but unapplied. We know better, but we do not work better because we tend to overlook or diminish items or tasks of importance. Fortunately for us, the chapters that follow provide guidance on the effective use of checklists and how to put them into practice to accomplish one of the most important goals of any organization—managing and optimizing people's potential. As Gawande indicates in the quote above, we must first acknowledge the indispensability of the tool and then put it into practice.

Common Uses and Errs

Checklists are most useful when they involve numerous or complex variables because they keep us from missing an important factor. However, they can be used for even the most mundane actions to cure forgetfulness or honest mistakes. It is easy to miss a critical step or element when activities have become so routine that they are habitual. Checklists are obviously invaluable when costly or deadly oversights are preventable, but even simple situations become difficult when we are under duress, in an emergency, or distracted. To err is human, so checklists must be used to protect against our own fallibilities.

Pause and Question

Checklists are ticklers in that they bring certain factors to our attention. According to Gawande, "pause points" allow us to question a situation so that we can make the right decision or take the right action.[39] Otherwise we might assume, operate automatically, or act on rote memory, which can all fail us sometimes. Humans are not computers and we do not operate or make decisions the same way all the time.

Performance Is an Art

Similarly, no one expects a singer to always perform the same way, and no teacher uses the exact same words or examples in every lecture of the same course. No athlete, regardless of her years of training, performs the same way every time she competes, even if she is a solo performer like a swimmer, gymnast, or sprinter. These athletes control almost all the variables, and yet no two performances are alike.

Things happen! Human performance is affected by everything from tools, equipment, the environment, and coworkers, to mood, attitude, the unpredictable, and chance. I have repeated a favorite saying from my experience counseling managers on planning for and reacting to personnel issues many, many times. The phrase is, "Human behavior is predictable, but individual behavior is not." We are sure that all people are fallible at some point, but we do not know when. Individual behavior varies and is unpredictable, so how can we assume a manager will be able to handle any type of difficult situation on the spot? Checklists can help account for dozens of variables that would be nearly impossible to keep on top of one's mind. It is even more challenging to stay in the moment when incidents are difficult, dangerous, excited, or emotional. While not a cure-all, checklists can ease the burden on one's mental faculties by acting as a tool, crutch, or resource for handling a situation.

Cheat Sheets, Checklists, and Ticklers

Simple management tools can be as effective as computers or machines when they help us take all considerations into account, and they make us mini experts when we follow their protocols. Cheat sheets, ticklers, and checklists compiled over a long period of time and prepared by experts and accomplished practitioners are wise and practical distillations of wisdom and experience. Why would any professional leave home or go to work without them? While following a checklist may not be a matter of grave importance to the average worker, the four examples outlined below will highlight how they can be the difference between life and death.

Checklists in Dire Action
Military Officers Use Checklists to Succeed in Battle

> *Laminate it, take it to the battlefield;*
> *it may save your life someday!*
> —U. S. Marine Officer maxim

Young Marines in infantry training digest a lot of material in a short amount of time, most of it with life or death consequences. These officers learn a great deal about leadership, ancient military skills, and ways of deploying what is known as the combat arts. Most importantly, they learn to make difficult decisions in a matter of seconds, many of which will be complicated, life-threatening, or lifesaving, and in the harshest of conditions—combat. These choices are consequential for the safety and survival of these officers and their fellow Marines.

Checklists are used for almost everything in the military, from cleaning one's weapon or completing a travel claim to more consequential matters like the four, life-saving steps. These essential first aid steps are so important they are learned by rote, as they must be quickly completed in the right order and without hesitation. "Stop the bleeding, start the breathing, protect the wound, treat for shock" is more than a mantra; these actions literally determine whether a fallen Marine goes from being injured in battle to the hospital or the morgue. If every Marine and soldier knows these words and the steps have been repeated so often in training that they have practically become a mantra, why is it necessary to write them down? They have been immortalized as a checklist precisely because they deal with mortal matters.

Checklists help ensure complete accuracy and proper sequencing for detailed and complicated matters like calling for firepower support from artillery or aircraft. The accuracy of these requests determines whether ordinance is delivered in a sufficient amount, and in time to neutralize the enemy threat, all within a margin of error of only a few hundred feet. A small mistake in the request can slow the response or incorrectly place the ordnances. They could not only miss the enemy target, but also land on the Marines themselves. A sample Call for Fire checklist is provided in Figure 14.1.

It is not often we give 22-year-olds the power, authority, and responsibility to make decisions that put as many as forty-two lives at stake every day. Yet, this is what is delegated to young Marine and Army Lieutenants. It is an awesome responsibility. Checklists help these bright, capable, courageous, and well-trained leaders perform at their highest level.

Write It Down, Save It, Update It, Treasure It

Military officers are given a variety of official checklists to use and follow. They are also repeatedly encouraged to keep, compile, and treasure their own personal collection of management and leadership tools. For Marine officers of my generation, it was called the Platoon Commander's Notebook.

CALL FOR FIRE CHECKLIST (Sample)	
1	REQUESTER ID: (Tack 29, this is Alpha 402)
2	WARNING ORDER
	Mission: Adjust fire, Fire for effect, Suppress
	Size: *(Omission indicates one battery volley)*
	Location Method: Grid, Polar, Shift
3.	TARGET LOCATION
	Grid: six digits
4.	TARGET DESCRIPTION
	Personnel, Armory, Structures, etc.
5	FIRE CONTROL
	Fire when ready; At my command; Time on target; Check fire

Figure 14.1. Call for Fire Checklist (Sample)

It was a small, handheld, two-ring binder that could be expanded or stuffed with tools, checklists, notes, and other important information. It was a ritual for senior officers training Marine lieutenants to say at the conclusion of instruction and upon the delivery of the all-important checklist, "Laminate it, take it to the battlefield; it may save your life someday." Lamination was needed to preserve the checklist and keep it from getting wet or destroyed. Saving this checklist to remember what to do in combat a year or two in the future might indeed save one's life.

Aviation Requires the Use of Checklists

> *For virtually everything that must be checked during a preflight, the pilot uses a written or electronic checklist. When you see a pilot using a checklist, you are seeing a professional approach to aviation. The few pilots who choose not to use these lists are risking some level of safety unless they are supremely-expert and have flawless memories.*
>
> —Matthew Johnston[40]

It is widely known in the aviation industry that the majority of catastrophes are the result of human error as opposed to mechanical failure. In fact, human mistakes account for 80% of crashes while the resulting 20% is attributable to equipment issues. Anyone who has boarded a commercial plane has witnessed not one, but two pilots seated in the cockpit reviewing long and elaborate checklists. These lists help ensure that all the systems in a complicated aircraft are prepared and ready to go.

While this mostly goes unseen by passengers, the pilot or copilot is also tasked with visually inspecting the aircraft. They look for structural problems that might not immediately register on their hundreds of sensors. It would be catastrophic for a tiny crack to appear and go unnoticed until it grew into a bigger problem. The structural integrity of the plane is most vulnerable during takeoff and landing, so discovering any type of irregularity is the priority of this visual inspection. I often feel sympathy for the copilot when flying in inclement weather because we all know who is inspecting the outside of the plane that day.

Everyone flying should hope that their pilots follow their prescribed checklists. It would be unconscionable for one's life to be put at risk because smart, capable, experienced, and expertly qualified people failed to follow simple instructions. Checklists are a guide, a check, and a double check. The hope is that pilots do not act upon their potential vanity and assume that they are too smart, capable, or experienced to heed a checklist. Our lives might depend on their assumptions or decision to follow a checklist.

Many Medical Errors Are Almost Predictable

One of the most fascinating yet disappointing books in the past decade is *The Checklist Manifesto* by Atul Gawande.[41] It makes simple and compelling arguments for why checklists are among the most valuable tools that humankind has ever created through fantastic stories. However, these tales are also deplorably disappointing. They demonstrate how countless medical errors are made every day, causing a loss of life or limb and untold other injuries because some of the brightest and best trained people alive today—surgeons and other medical professionals—have committed negligent errors. Some of their reprehensible errors are as simple as not washing their hands and therefore spreading germs that kill their patients.

The Checklist Manifesto has become somewhat of a movement. There is a cadre of professionals, hospitals, and national and international health organizations campaigning for the mandatory use of checklists during any medical procedure or surgery in hospitals and clinics. How could smart and educated people not follow simple instructions like washing their hands? It can be summarized into two simple words: human error. Sometimes it is forgetfulness and an honest mistake, but it can also be arrogance, contempt, vanity, or willful and professional neglect. Unfortunately, for inexplicable reasons, medical professionals trained to double check one another often do not follow through on the practice.

The most dramatic medical errors end up on the evening news. We have all seen X-rays of scalpels, needles, scissors, or sponges left inside of people's bodies after a surgery. An extremely simple checklist that directs the medical team to take specific actions before and after surgery could prevent almost 100% of these errors; see Figure 14.2 for an example. However, Gawande reports that such errors are made about 5,000 times a year.[42] One early study of checklists in hospitals showed that there was a 36% reduction in medical complications after surgery and a 47% reduction in deaths after the introduction of checklists.

Checklist: Hemodialysis Catheter Connection
- ☐ Wear mask (if required)
- ☐ Perform hand hygiene
- ☐ Put on new, clean gloves
- ☐ Clamp the catheter and remove caps
- ☐ Scrub catheter hub with antiseptic
- ☐ Allow hub antiseptic to dry
- ☐ Connect catheter to blood lines aseptically
- ☐ Remove gloves
- ☐ Perform hand hygiene

Figure 14.2. Hemodialysis Catheter Connection Checklist. *Developed by the Making Dialysis Safer for Patients Coalition and the Centers for Disease Control and Prevention, National Center for Emerging and Zoonotic Infectious Diseases.*

One could argue that many medical errors are not mistakes at all; they are predictable outcomes of a flawed system, one that assumes human beings are infallible. We allow teams of surgeons and medical professionals to work from memory and experience, a good and reasonable practice because they are well-trained and practiced in their field. Yet, who would want to bet their life on the chance that their surgical team were not human that day and could not make a potentially fatal mistake?

Emergency and Safety Checklists

All around us are examples of what to do when there are crises, large and small. Almost every guide we are given on how to prepare for or act during an emergency includes some form of a checklist. They are invaluable emergency aids whether we are advised by the government to prepare for inclement weather by keeping a hurricane or blizzard preparation checklist at home, directed by our employer to prepare for a workplace safety event, or trained on proper exit protocol in the event of a fire. Some lists tell us to stock up on flashlights, batteries, milk, and bread, or put extra clothing in the trunk of our cars in case we are stranded. Regardless of the topic, checklists help us prepare for both the expected and unexpected.

If you live within fifty miles of a nuclear energy plant or own a boat for leisure, you will have checklists. Nuclear plants provide the public with instructions on what to do if there is a spill, the Coast Guard provides boaters with vessel safety checklists, and the Girl Scouts provide packing lists for campers. A travel or camping checklist might not appear to be imperative, but they could be lifesaving if one has a severe allergic reaction to a bee sting and the packing list included an EpiPen.

Checklists in Performance Conversations

The argument for the Performance Conversations Checklist approach is that while one's life might not be at stake in the workplace, one's livelihood could when performance is discussed. Employment, careers, professional development, pay, promotions, and other factors are affected by performance discussions, so we will discuss in the pages that follow why using checklists is a reasonable idea worth consideration.

15

Performance Conversations Checklists: Putting the Technique into Action

Much like questions, checklists have tremendous utility and are everywhere. They are usually presented linearly or as a list of prompts or questions. Check to see if the valve is open, verify you are receiving a signal, call for assistance if the problem persists. Did you remember to turn off the stove, heater, iron, light, safety valve, and so on before you left the room? Is the green light flashing to indicate the system is operating properly? Is there enough space between the two items? Whether the checklist is a set of instructions for operating a machine, a troubleshooting guide, or a list of reminders, it ensures a procedure is followed.

They can act as cheat sheets to help someone learn or ticklers that prompt us to take some future action. Checklists help us remember to do things in a certain way every time. If they are indispensable to professionals operating complex equipment or conducting high risk procedures, like pilots and surgeons, why shouldn't managers consider using them before performing the delicate art of conducting a performance conversation with an employee?

It seems like checklists are everywhere except regular professional work environments like the boardroom, meeting room, or supervisor's office. While there are many complex facilities to manage, like nuclear power plants, advance manufacturing environments, robotics labs, and industrial maintenance businesses, there is one thing that is more intricate—human beings. People are unpredictable and have variables and patterns that demand our attention, skill, empathy, engagement, follow-through, and focus. This book argues that checklists are a superior tool for managing people, especially during the performance improvement process.

A Checklist for All Accounts

The Performance Conversations Checklist approach accomplishes three primary objectives related to performance improvement: account for a large number of performance variables, hold the manager and employee accountable to these factors, and ensure that priority tasks are accomplished within a defined period.

A Performance Conversations Checklist is a valuable quality assurance tool when managing the unique priorities of any organization, department, or team. The checklist requires the manager and employee communicate, consider, and act on consequential matters. For example, a checklist prompt might remind a manager to review an employee's compensation once a year. It would not require that an employee's pay change, only that the manager reconsider the amount, check with HR, or compare it with peers. The last thing a manager would want is for a great employee to leave the organization for a small pay difference. The checklist ensures that a manager remains aware of this variable and can act if necessary.

A checklist might also prompt an employee to take specific actions, like updating their goals for the year. Including a semiannual professional or career development item in a Performance Conversations Checklist would demand that the participants discuss the employee's potential interests and training needs. The number of checklist improvement variables one could include is endless. The challenge is ensuring the checklist is a tailored list of the most important factors related to one's work, not a laundry list of anything possible. Every environment will be different, so it is important to curate the checklist to address specific needs.

Not Everything All of the Time

A Performance Conversations Checklist needs to include a time variable. After accounting for everything that should be tracked, monitored, and managed, it is necessary to determine when and how often a factor is reviewed. Some activities should be discussed at every performance conversation, others quarterly, and some only annually. For example, one might need to update job descriptions once a year, consider retention biannually, or, if morale is a high priority, give kudos to staff each quarter. Many would argue that all organizations, both profit and non-profit, should include revenue-generating or cost-saving strategies on performance lists as well. The checklist is then a catalog of important matters, a prompt, a tracking device, and a time management tool, all without building another system to accommodate these needs.

A manager can tend to about a dozen variables from a single piece of paper with the Performance Conversations Checklist technique, as seen in Appendix N. A simple to-do list informs the manager on what needs to be addressed, provides options for the future, and reminds him or her to complete specific tasks within a given time frame. This can all be accomplished with a basic spreadsheet, table, or grid. The rows contain topics to be discussed or addressed, and the columns suggest which quarter such items can be reviewed. The KISS principle states it best—keep it simple, stupid.

The frequent checking in characteristic of the Performance Conversations method helps the technique avoid the pitfalls of traditional appraisals, where one attempts to force a year's worth of management into a single meeting. This flexible method also allows items to be spread and managed over the year, tracked over time, and accomplished or reviewed when necessary, all on a single piece of paper. There is beauty in its simplicity.

The tickler system built into the checklist allows many situations to develop organically, like discussing career development in the summer because many people like to start academic programs in the fall. Additionally, a manager might be prompted to compliment an employee's efforts if the row for recognition is empty after a year. Every employee is likely to have performed well at something over a year's time, and providing recognition is believed to be an essential ingredient for high workplace engagement. On the flip side, it can be telling if the box for attaching documentary evidence of the completion of good work is blank.

The simple listing of an organization's major performance variables on one page is a great reminder of what is important. The presence and absence of checkmarks become powerful performance indicators for both the employee and the manager. However, not every task has to be managed at once. The frequency built into the Performance Conversations method allows all things to be considered and completed in due time.

The What and Why of Appraisals

The biggest challenge and failure of traditional performance appraisal systems is that they do not know why they exist and many of their purposes are at odds. They are purportedly designed to improve performance, but documenting past action is not correlated with better execution in the future. Other fundamental flaws include their ratings, poor design, and failure to account for human fallibility (e.g. a manager's potential inability to rate fairly). Every major 20th-century performance appraisal framework undermined its own effectiveness by making the wrong assumptions, promoting unrealistic fallacies, and relying too heavily on the judgement of supervisors. One must know the goals of traditional appraisal systems and why they are popular for management before designing a better alternative. Clarity is a precursor to success.

As an example, many traditional appraisal systems claimed to be performance *management* systems when they were really designed to evaluate performance history. The assumption was that rating the past would prompt people to perform better in the future. However, ample evidence shows that this technique often demotivated the people it was designed to support. Additionally, organizations repeatedly misled their employees. They claimed performance appraisals were about encouraging improvement, when really, they were a compensation determination tool. Appraisals decided who got a raise and ratings were tucked away in a file without follow-up training and development.

Finally, everyone knows that any manager worthy of his or her position manipulated the ratings to get the management end necessary for success. Ratings were inflated to motivate poor performing employees hypersensitive to negative feedback or retain average employees thinking about leaving the organization in a tight job market. Unfortunately, according to countless studies and reports, managers also used ratings to play favorites and unfairly assess those of a different race, gender, nationality, or alma mater. There were good ideas behind some of these schemata, but ultimately, they were poorly executed.

This Is Not "PC"

Before listing and defining the plethora of purposes for performance management, it is worth noting that the Performance Conversations method is not designed to be a traditional performance management tool—it is a performance improvement system. This might seem like semantics, but it is not. The Performance Conversations method is future-oriented and focused on productivity—period! It is not "consultant-speak," or a politically correct rephrasing of old ways of thinking and working.

Remember that the building blocks for the Performance Conversations method are different from traditional appraisals. Table 15.1 provides some quick examples. Some have already been discussed previously in the text, but many others will be explained in the pages that follow.

While Table 15.1 is not exhaustive, it should be illustrative. Performance Conversations are designed to help people get and feel better about their work. Improving requires a coach willing to lead and an employee willing to learn. It demands dialogue, questioning, understanding, changing, problem-solving, direction, forecasting, supporting, and monitoring. Feeling better stems from rapport, encouragement, reflection, positivity, collaboration, and other characteristics of one's relationship with a manager. Never before have the words learning, encouraging, and positivity been associated with performance appraisals.

Table 15.1. Premises, Purposes, and Practices: Performance Conversations vs. Traditional Appraisals

Performance Conversations®	Traditional Appraisals
Conversation	Evaluation
Two-way dialogue	One-way communication of results or ratings
Coach	Judge
Coaching to improve	Directing
No ratings	Ratings
Future-oriented	Past-oriented
Feedback and feedforward	Feedback and constructive criticism
Co-performance	Individual performs while supervisor monitors
Partnership	Power Relationship
Efforts, Outcomes, Behaviors	Outcomes and some behaviors
Evidence and artifacts	Memory and documentation
Performance logs (employee and manager)	Supervisor's file
Check-in conversations	Annual review
Multiple thirty-minute conversations	Annual review
Real-time feedback and adjustment	End of year adjustment

Efforts, Outcomes, and Behaviors: The Superior Mix of Performance Conversations

Lest critics argue that Performance Conversations are weak versions of appraisals designed to be all talk and no substance, it is worth reiterating that Performance Conversations are designed to manage the whole performance. The holistic concept of efforts, outcomes, and behaviors was introduced in *Performance Conversations: An Alternative to Appraisals.* The book reminded readers that most appraisal systems are only focused on outcomes, or the quality and quantity of results. A few tracked behaviors, and far fewer even paid homage to the idea of effort. Yet, the Performance Conversations method accounts for all three.

Outcomes and results are easy to track, manage, and discuss, and many employees appear exceptional when these are the only factors considered. However, when behavior is introduced, some superstars become average. These are the highfliers who work well alone but are not good teammates, and they poison the work environment. An A+ in sales and a D+ in relations with others gets you a B- rating in organizations smart enough to evaluate collegiality, collaboration, teamwork, and inclusion. Adding efforts to the mix provides an even greater level of accountability. Efforts are acting professional, working hard, staying safe, following procedure, and trying to do the right thing. Some people simply refuse to play nice (behavior) or play fair (efforts).

The example of a B- rating mentioned above was for instructional purposes only as ratings are not used in the Performance Conversations method. The point is that employees are held to task in Performance Conversations by their actions, methods, and ability to work well with others. In a Performance Conversations world, one cannot be a superstar unless they have good outcomes, great relationships, and they do the right thing, the right way. This is the ultimate accountability.

Ratings are not necessary to achieving these ends, and traditional appraisals miss these points all together because efforts and behaviors are often not even considered. Furthermore, they often try to account for every possible performance variable, which is impossible. As a result, many contain a laundry list of "performance dimensions" and an exhausting number of items. Finally, there are three purposes of most performance management systems that are often misunderstood and misapplied. These traditional goals can be summarized as feedback, accountability, and growth.

What Are the Purposes of Performance Management Anyway?

Here is a quick summary of the most prominent purposes of performance management found in management literature over the last seventy years, even though performance management has not lived up to these purposes and they are not practiced in reality.

- **Accountability**: Ensure work is completed correctly; admonishment or punishment when necessary.
- **Administrative**: Determine compensation, promotions, training or leadership program eligibility, layoff order, and countless other reasons related to employment.
- **Evaluation**: Rate the quality of performance.
- **Feedback**: Provide information regarding the quality and quantity of work performed.
- **Goal Management**: Track and manage goals, plans, and projects.
- **Growth/Development**: Learning and career development, as needed.
- **Improvement**: The Holy Grail that was never achieved and attempted rarely by design.
- **Managing Performance**: Track, monitor, and adjust performance.
- **Motivating Good Performance**: Assumption that ratings inspire more or better performance.
- **Ranking**: Align employees in order of success, often to determine raises, promotability, etc.
- **Rating**: Assign a performance score relative to coworkers and/or an organizational standard.
- **Record Keeping**: Document past performance.
- **Strategic**: Align efforts with organizational objectives or teammates.

This is not a master list, but an overview of the typical performance management purposes found in workplaces across the globe.

Most systems failed in their design. They tried to accomplish almost everything listed above using a form. The creators (consultants and HR pros) and the users (managers) were rightfully confused. Even when their purposes were narrow and clear, the system designs were nonsensical. You cannot create a fixed form that can manage all the objectives listed above, all the time, for all types of jobs in different departments of a company. Any system designed to evaluate vice presidents, accountants, custodians, and information technology professionals is probably so generic that it is ineffectual for every position.

Traditional appraisal and most performance management systems designed in the 20th century did not work. So, in the 21st century, we need better tools. Fortunately, one or two (okay, three) have been introduced in this book.

Performance Conversations Are Not One-on-One Meetings, Per Se

Similar to the explanation regarding the difference between performance appraisals and our performance improvement system, there are a few caveats and disclaimers worth noting here. One-on-one meetings are generally designed to support individuals and their work, regardless of whether implicitly or explicitly stated. It is easy to consider someone's external work performance; however, as noted in earlier chapters, we must manage both the performer and *person* behind the performance. Traditional performance appraisals are destructive, as they tear people down as oppose to building them up—boosting confidence.

New performance management systems designed in recent years all focus on the individual through one-on-one meetings in some way because they are designed to be interactive and to include the employee as a full participant. This objective is included implicitly, but few consciously acknowledge the underlying principle that the discussion is about the employee as a whole being—person and performer. It matters what Bob thinks, and Shalita's performance will improve if her boss thanks her for doing things outside of her job, like helping coworkers with their deadlines without being asked. When Chen stops and takes a few moments to talk about Julio's aspiration to get a master's degree it makes Julio feel appreciated. He is then more engaged in his work and becomes determined to perform at the highest level possible while he is in graduate school to show his appreciation for Chen's support.

The caveat is that Performance Conversations are not just generic one-on-one meetings in disguise. They are planned, structured, and purposeful discussions operated within a framework. Performance Conversations are part of a performance improvement system, one with supporting foundational theories, a descriptive model, and a series of proven management practices. Performance Conversations are more than a simple meeting.

Performance Conversations Purposes and Practices

The Performance Conversations method is a framework that uses conversations to promote a series of positive outcomes and improve performance. It is designed to coach an employee toward greater success, develop their skills, and encourage and support their overall professional wellbeing. Our mantra is to help employees get better, do better, and feel better about work. The practices and objectives listed below all support these ends.

- **Accountability**: To hold one responsible for their progress, success, missteps, or mistakes.
- **Affirmation**: To let employees know that they are on the right path and doing the right things.
- **Alignment**: To ensure efforts are consistent with others and organizational goals.
- **Career Development**: To discuss the future, give advice, and identify skill-building or advancement opportunities.
- **Coaching**: To focus on individual development, performance, and wellbeing.
- **Development/Growth**: To discuss formal and informal opportunities to learn and grow.
- **Feedback**: To provide information, observation, or data regarding past efforts, outcomes, and behaviors.
- **Feedforward**: To envision efforts and interventions to make improvements.
- **Investment**: To expend time and effort in support of employee engagement, success, and retention.
- **Problem Resolution**: To remove obstacles to good performance.
- **Promotability**: To determine employee interest and potential in taking on new assignments.
- **Performance Improvement**: To uncover ways of working better, smarter, or faster.
- **Rapport**: To build the relationship and partnership between the manager and employee (coach and performer).

- **Recognition**: To acknowledge an employee's progress or success with kudos, compliments, or thanks.
- **Reflection**: To gain insight by reviewing or assessing past efforts.
- **Retention**: To remind employees that they are valued, appreciated, and vital to the team.

Table 15.2 provides the proof and consistency of purpose for the Performance Conversations method.

While the purposes and practices of the model are extensive and different from the norm, they are largely positive, easy to understand, and the coaching approach naturally advances all these goals. Additionally, the Magnificent Seven Questions cover almost all these factors directly or indirectly so following that technique is like one-stop shopping for performance improvement. A checklist can tally and check off each of these topics over time, which is important to consider as it is not possible or reasonable to cover all these objectives at once. The frequency factor in the

Table 15.2. Performance Conversations Goals and Activities

Get Better	Perform Better	Feel Better
	Accountability	
	Alignment	
		Affirmation
Career development		
Coaching	Coaching	Coaching
Development	Development	
Feedback	Feedback	Feedback
Feedforward	Feedforward	
Investment	Investment	
	Problem resolution	
Promotability		Promotability
Performance improvement	Performance improvement	Performance improvement
	Rapport	Rapport
	Recognition	Recognition
Reflection	Reflection	
		Retention

model also includes conversation to address all these topics, as necessary. This is made easier in the Performance Conversations model as it offers four to twelve opportunities instead of a single high-stakes conversation held once a year.

Now That We Know What We're Doing, Let's Talk about How to Do It

Having some clarity about what we hope to accomplish—to help employees get better, do better, and feel better—can help build the system needed to achieve our goals. They can all be secured over time by using a checklist to track, monitor, and manage the support activities necessary to bring them to life. Simple versions of tracking sheets can be developed and used within the Performance Conversations Checklist approach. There is no preferred format, form, or superior instrument, and a bulleted list of the highest priorities to discuss, track, and manage would be suitable for most work environments. It does not have to be complicated. Try out this sample email as an easy way to cover all the purposes and practices of a performance conversation session:

Sample Performance Conversations Checklist Letter

Dear ____:

We will meet every other month for half an hour to discuss the aspects of our business with the greatest impact. The goal of these conversations is ensuring that the work is done well, that you are happy and fulfilled with your work, and that the business thrives. Any, and all, of your thoughts, ideas, and opinions matter.

Come prepared to talk about any of these topics that may be needed or timely:

- Customer satisfaction
- Product quality and quantity
- Improvement ideas
- Concerns you have about assignments, others, etc.
- Tools or resources you need to succeed
- Other things you want to talk about

We will discuss any questions you may have when we meet.

What else is needed in a small business with three dozen employees, a company with 400, or even a corporation with 4,000? The idea is to talk with people about the most important work variables, identify their obstacles to good performance, and then act to address these challenges.

Forget the form, follow the process. If you focus on improvement and incorporate the fabulous five principles—feedback, feedforward, frequency, follow-up, and familiarity—all will be well. Now, let us practice the method in real time. Here is a quality control checklist for creating a Performance Conversations Checklist:

- ☐ **Step 1:** Create a list of the things that matter most for the business, department, team, and/or individuals involved.
- ☐ **Step 2:** Develop a list of prompts or questions designed to get employees to think about the topics and prepare for the check-in.
- ☐ **Step 3:** Review the Performance Conversations purpose list above to see if you are missing any objectives important to your business (e.g. recognition, career planning, retention, etc.). Then, incorporate a prompt or question to address the new items. For example, if retention is an issue at your business, you might ask "What do you like about working here at _____?" A celebration (or recognition) item is a great reminder for you to give kudos to an employee and allows them to highlight an accomplishment of which they are especially proud.
- ☐ **Step 4:** Refine the list of topics or questions and create a one-page or less form to give to the manager and employee. It will help them know what information they need to prepare and discuss when they meet.
- ☐ **Step 5:** Send staff the one-page form and ask them to add topics they consider relevant and to think about the objectives before the next meeting. (You can also tell them they are encouraged to bring any documents, artifacts, or evidence of well-done work if they want.)
- ☐ **Step 6:** Schedule a series of short meetings with each employee to exchange information and share feedback and feedforward with your staff.
- ☐ **Step 7:** Relax, go to the meeting, and engage with the employee using the form as a guide. Remember: the conversation is the main event, not the form.

That's it. Congratulations, you have nearly mastered the Performance Conversations Checklist technique by following a few simple steps, in the form of a checklist, of course.

A THIRTY-MINUTE CONVERSATION

16

A Thirty-Minute Conversation: Can We Talk about Our Work Together?

The goal of every interaction between a manager and an employee should be performance improvement. The manager's goal should be to help staff get better, perform better, and feel better about their work—this is coaching at its best. As stated earlier, a manager is just unnecessary if they do not help the employee perform at a higher level than what he or she would alone. Both great coaches and great managers help others learn, grow, develop, and improve their personal and professional skills—get better. They help others put new knowledge, skills, and abilities into action—perform better. Moreover, they help others understand and appreciate the importance, value, and impact of what they have done—feel better. This appreciation increases employee desire, willingness, and commitment to continuously perform well over time—engagement.

Management and performance management are two sides of the same coin. Managers should be responsible for the whole system—tracking, managing, assessing, and improving performance. When the Human Resources department is in charge of performance management and managers are in charge of managing performance, there are bound to be disconnections between what is expected and what actually occurs. Performance does not stop in December and then restart in January. Business is ongoing. There are no finish lines, just weigh stations along the way to pause, reflect, adjust, refuel, and continue. The question is, "How can we accomplish the goals of management and performance management together?" If one's ultimate goal is performance improvement, the answer can be found within these pages.

The thirty-minute conversation has the added benefit of being all about the employee and what he or she needs to succeed. Experience tells us that employees revel in the opportunity to get their supervisor's undivided attention during the hectic pace of work. Actions are paused for a moment or two and the focus is turned to helping improve the employee's performance. When planned and executed well, this dedicated time can plant seeds that will flower into better future performance.

Preparing for a Performance Conversation
Preparation Is Supreme

The best meetings are planned and have an agenda and specific outcome in mind. Performance Conversations are no different. The Performance Questions technique streamlines and simplifies the effective meeting process, the Performance Conversations Checklist ensures that no stone is left unturned, and the classic Performance Portfolio is best suited for when artifacts and evidence are collected and needed to describe, define, or diagnose the quality of work being performed. They all have their own protocol and the questions, checklists, and logs are used as agenda. The goals or outcomes sought are obvious—performance improvement.

Preparation Instruments

Preparation materials can be used to jumpstart good conversations. A single sheet of paper listing the Magnificent Seven Questions will suffice (Appendix H provides an example). The employee and manager can review the list in advance and think about their answers to those questions. If they realize that they do not have a good answer to a question, they will act to gather information, produce evidence, or otherwise prepare to address the gap in data before or during the meeting. Developing a series of questions about the priorities, challenges, and opportunities associated with work and then reviewing the list in advance creates an easy preparation checklist. Any questions focused on the most important aspects of work can be useful and used repeatedly; Appendices A–G provide excellent examples.

More formal tools can be developed to equip the employee and manager for their conversations. Preparation instruments that reflect local considerations can be designed as well. These tools can be topical and address specific areas of importance to the company; goal-oriented by focusing on performance targets and action plans; checklist-oriented by delineating work requirements, such as required discussions about strategy, operations, position descriptions, or policies and procedures; or operational regarding the efforts, activities, and behaviors that drive major work processes. The design options are limitless. The only requirement for a preparation instrument is that it reflects the highest priorities of a performance improvement discussion.

Sample preparation instruments are provided in Appendices H–M. Regardless of the performance conversation method chosen—Portfolio, Question, or Checklist—it is prudent to prepare for the conversation. Just as athletes practice before big games or thespians conduct rehearsals, preparing for a performance conversation can only make it better. Preparation also helps ensure that these discussions are conducted and concluded in the allotted time period.

To Hold or Not to Hold (This Is the Question When You Are Not Prepared)

Regardless of our good intentions, there will undoubtedly come a time when we are simply not prepared to hold a performance conversation. Here is a suggested protocol of what to do when either you or the employee is not prepared:

If the manager is unprepared:

1. Hold the meeting, allow the employee to ask more questions than normal, and share the information and materials they have collected.
2. Reschedule the meeting until another day.

If the employee is unprepared:

1. Delay the meeting for fifteen minutes and have the employee leave and reflect upon past efforts and prepare for the meeting. Hold the meeting in the time remaining when they return.
2. Hold the meeting and have the manager lead the discussion and pose a series of questions designed to gather a complete work status report.
3. Reschedule the meeting until another day.

If both the manager and employee are unprepared:

1. Hold the meeting and use the Magnificent Seven Questions, a generic list of questions, a preparation instrument, or other prompt to guide the conversation anyway
2. Delay the meeting fifteen minutes and have the employee and manager use that time to reflect upon recent work and come back prepared to discuss within the time available.
3. Asking the first three questions of the Magnificent Seven will suffice as a shorthand method of holding a performance conversation.
4. Reschedule the meeting until another day.

One of the advantages of the structured and planned nature of Performance Conversations is that it allows adjustments if necessary. If the interval established for conversations is every six weeks (or eight per year) and circumstances prevent a meeting from occurring, the beauty is that there are still seven other feedback opportunities that year. While it is best to postpone instead of skip meetings, the structure inherent to Performance Conversations allows some leeway.

On the same note, a major faux pas is to cancel two meetings in a row because it signals that the conversations are not important. While things might get busy and holding conversations might rightfully become a distraction from urgent, pressing, real work, a pattern of missed meetings says more about the manager's time management ability than it does anything else. One strategy is to not cancel the second meeting in a row and reschedule instead. Even if the second meeting is rescheduled three times, this still says to the employee that this conversation is so important that you will do everything you can to keep it from being canceled.

In Due Time—Holding to the Schedule
When Employees Request to Cancel or Postpone Conversations

Another advantage of the Performance Conversations method is that accountability is subtly built into the process. Good employees might delay a meeting because they are not prepared to share all their successful work in an intelligible manner. They want to make a positive showing, which is precisely why they are good employees. Other times, they are far too busy, in a groove, and just want to continue working. This is also an acceptable delay.

Well- and poor-performing employees alike sometimes do not want to have a face-to-face, one-on-one conversation because they know they will have to admit to something, discuss a problem, or disclose an obstacle. Sometimes, the Performance Conversations method makes it easier to diagnose a problem and intervene faster than usual. A previously scheduled, bimonthly performance conversation requires an employee to disclose that they *think* they will miss their quarterly goals before the goal is missed. The manager then has the option of intervening and providing support, assistance, or additional resources so that the objective can still be accomplished. Asking "What is not going well?", "What else is going on?", and "What is the status of your goals?" compels employees to discuss their problems.

Managers should notice and act when an employee wants to postpone or cancel a conversation. Before agreeing, a manager might say, "Yes, provided that you do not know of any problems or issues that are time sensitive." Alternatively, the manager might ask, "Are there any problems that we can cover now and then delay discussing other matters?" Either way, changes to previously planned meetings can be an early indicator of problems or obstacles.

Bad News Does Not Get Better with Age
At some point during the game of work, there will be problems, challenges, mistakes, or bad behavior. As time passes, the behavior, misunderstandings, or bad habits may crystallize, harden, and become engrained, maybe even fester. So, act today!

One of the limitations of traditional appraisals is that managers are reluctant to give critical feedback because truthfully, it is difficult to do. While not explicitly acknowledged in the management literature, every supervisor knows how hard it is to sit across the table from another person and deliver bad news or critiques, or tell them that they made a big mistake. If it were easy, it would happen more often.

If negative feedback is given along with instruction and support (coaching) in a timely fashion, the employee can immediately make a positive change and correct the issue. This is analogous to a star quarterback being told that they did a poor job in the first quarter of the game or a headlining actor learning they made mistakes during the first act of a play. The person can then take this criticism and change to win the game or improve the performance. It would be futile to wait until the end of the game or after the final act to share negative feedback.

Practice Makes Perfect Performance Conversations
Difficult Conversations Made Easier

> *A good question can be like an elixir that softens*
> *a bad mood, melts anger, and pulls the other*
> *person back to the truly important issues.*
> —Andrew Sobel and Jerald Panas[43]

It is hard to have a difficult conversation, no doubt, but here are a few tips to conducting them well. First, prepare. Be clear on what is wrong and what needs to be said. Writing down these ideas is good advice. Second, plan. Think about how, when, and where the information can and should be delivered. This is essential to communicating the importance and gravity of the issue at hand. Should one have someone sit in on the meeting? Should one offer the employee an opportunity to have a witness or supporter? Should the meeting be held in one's office, a conference room, or over a lunch offsite? For most routine negative feedback situations designed to improve work, such efforts are unnecessary or inappropriate, yet this sort of forethought is important to determining how to complete this second step. Third, practice. A good approach is to write down the opening lines of a hard conversation. This helps reduce the difficulty of the discussion, ease nervousness, and improve the delivery of critical information because it is easy to bungle a remark when the stakes are high. The matter can be made worse if a heated word is used instead of one more benign. The words "inappropriate" versus "disgraceful" or "problem" versus "issue" will likely get different responses. Most employees would be insulted if their work were called "mediocre" when the word "average" would have communicated the same information. Writing down and reading the first or critical words when providing negative feedback is an insurance policy against verbal blunders and miscommunication.

The final, critical piece of advice is to not assume that the issue will be resolved at the end of the conversation. Experience indicates that sometimes the first meeting is only filled with shock, denial, resistance, and possibly even anger. The receiver may not like, agree, or appreciate the negative feedback, but you cannot force someone to understand or like what they hear. So, do not force the issue. Let it sit and return to the matter later. Say what needs to be said, do not engage in a prolonged debate about the matter, and please, do not argue or fight about it! The manager's judgment will ultimately prevail the vast majority of the time.

One-, Two-, or Three-Meeting Conversations

Do not push or attempt to require someone to agree with the content of the negative information. Take a ten- or fifteen-minute break and then resume the conversation later to let tensions and emotions wane. Maybe, let it lie for a day or two and plan another meeting to continue the discussion. Experience foretells that there are one-, two-, and three-meeting difficult conversations. Depending upon the content, a seasoned manager will likely be able to anticipate how many meetings a conversation may take. Human Resources professionals can be helpful in making this determination as well. Ultimately, difficult conversations should be brief and factual—fifteen minutes is a good guide. Separating critical communications into parts, or providing difficult to swallow feedback in small doses is helped when two or three meetings are planned.

Listen More, Talk Less

One of the best techniques for holding a good performance discussion with staff members is to listen more than one talks. Questions facilitate this goal. An added benefit is that the employee knows they will get half an hour in the sun when the meeting is focused on them. Most would likely be pleased knowing they will get their manager's undivided attention for this brief period.

There are many benefits to listening, without many disadvantages, but it can be bungled as easily as asking questions the wrong way. A few examples of listening faux pas are interrupting someone while they are speaking, ignoring their response, acting or appearing distracted while they are speaking, or otherwise not giving them one's complete and courteous attention.

Delivery: How You Say It

> *The manner of the question, the way in which it is asked,*
> *and the actual communication of the question are all*
> *just as important as the substance of the question.*
>
> —Terry Fadem[44]

Needless to say, how you say what you say is important. Some communications experts argue that as much as 70% of communication is nonverbal. The tone, pronunciation, pace, and octave of our voices, as well as our facial expression and body language reveal much about what is communicated. Despite great preparation and intent, questions can be bungled on delivery. This should not be of great concern if the climate is positive, the relationship between the manager and employee is solid, and the collaboration between the two is sound. With these conditions the words and how they are delivered will matter less. Even if you are ineloquent in the delivery, the messages that you and the employee are a team and you will figure it out together are more important.

So, relax and have a positive conversation. Good advice for all circumstances includes making eye contact, smiling at the appropriate time, leaning forward to show interest, and never folding one's arms. A word of caution would be appropriate, however. If one is not genuine about wanting to have a non-evaluative feedback conversation designed to support the employee and improve performance, one will likely not succeed because the lack of authenticity will be obvious. This is probably one of the reasons traditional appraisals fail. They are often predicated upon an artificial environment of power and judgment created for a single hour, once a year, and it undermines the previous relationship and spirit of cooperation that existed between the manager and employee 99.9% of the other time. If you have good intentions of helping the employee and do not judge, the right words will come out naturally.

Templates and Tools
Prompts, Crutches, Templates, and Survival Techniques

Developing good questions takes work. However,
some shortcuts exist. Keeping a list of questions
around to help you in many different kinds
of business settings might prove useful.

—Terry Fadem[45]

The magic of the Performance Conversations method is in the interactive one-on-one meeting and the relationship between two partners working together toward common goals. International diplomacy, legal proceedings, marital counseling sessions, and other challenging human situations are most successful when the parties involved agree to talk, that is, to engage in healthy dialogue. However, what happens when you are stuck? Prompts, go-to questions, templates, and other techniques can help when the conversation becomes stalled or derailed.

Opening Lines

It is advisable to develop a series of opening lines, introductory remarks, or useful phrases to start conversations on the right note. One idea is to remind the employee of the purpose of the conversation at the beginning of the meeting as a quality assurance technique and to ensure that the meeting is focused. Statements like the following can be useful:

- "Of course, we are meeting again to talk about the most important aspects of work. Our goal is to figure out how to identify those that are going well so that they can be repeated, disclose and discuss problems so that we can adjust, and share information that might otherwise be useful in our work together."
- "Let's talk about our highest priorities, the biggest challenges, and what we have to get done by _____. If we concentrate on these issues first, we can save time at the end for a general discussion on everything else."
- "The goal of this conversation is to ensure your success and that I am doing everything I can to help you perform your best every day. So, regardless of the questions asked, let's make sure we keep this in mind."

Writing down the opening words in advance and reading them verbatim is good advice and a smart practice.

Other effective ways of starting a conversation with a goal in mind are to use opening lines that follow up from previous conversations or address difficult issues. Opening lines can also establish rapport and help build the right relationship to encourage open, honest, and forthright business conversations. If the employee does not feel good about the relationship, they may not feel good about the conversation. They are likely to be less engaged, forthcoming, and cooperative in the dialogue.

Two other easy opening lines can be asking a specific and narrow question regarding work items where the employee is already known to be successful, or giving the employee kudos for a project that has gone well. This relaxes both parties and allows the conversation to ease into matters that are more difficult. In all circumstances, getting off to a good start is critical to the success of the conversation. Three final examples of opening lines are included below:

- "The last time we met, we had two things that needed to be completed before this meeting. What has occurred since then?"
- "The work on _____ was not up to our standards of excellence. We must figure out how to prevent that from happening again. Let's talk about what we can do together to make all the things we do a success."
- "I hope that you're doing okay. For me, these past few weeks have been hectic. However, that's no excuse because we have important work to do. How are you feeling? Are you ready to tackle the _____? We need to complete our goals by summer."

Template Questions and Topics

Template questions can serve as great placeholders or prompts for those occasions when words and ideas are not coming as easily as one would prefer. To avoid long pauses, awkward silence, or fumbled questions, keep a reserve of generic, proven questions and use specific conversational techniques. Some of these include asking the employee to provide more information on one or more topics; explain what has already been discussed; summarize what has been said; give their opinion on an important matter in the past, present or future; or talk about the future.

Tell Me More
- "Can you tell me more about that?"
- "You said _____; would you give me more information about it?"
- "That sounds interesting, what else happens with that?"

Explain
- "Can you explain that in detail for me?"
- "What do you mean when you say _____?"
- "What does _____ mean to you?"

Summarize
- "Would you summarize _____ so that I am sure I understand what you meant?"
- "We have talked about a number of things today, what do you think was most important?"
- "What would be a good overview statement that describes what we are talking about?"

Offer an Opinion
- "What are your thoughts about how we have organized the work?"
- "Do you think that there are better ways of accomplishing _____?"
- "If you were to recommend a new brand of _____ for us to consider, what would it be?"
- "Have you ever thought about _____?"

Assess Feelings
- "How do you feel about how things are going?"
- "Are things going okay lately?"
- "Are things at work up to your level of satisfaction?"

Future
- "What are your highest priorities for next week?"
- "What should we plan to do for the remainder of this year?"
- "What do you think will be the changes in our industry in the next five years?"

Prompts, crutches, and templates are also effective tools to use when you are stuck or when the conversation goes awry, becomes hostile, or is otherwise not going well. Tony Stoltzfus, the author of *Coaching Questions*, believes that one of the best techniques is to ask the other person the simple question, "Can we start over?"[46] A preface to clarify the situation or to restate your good intent might also help the situation. Additional alternative phrasings may include questions and statements such as the following:

- "My goal for the conversation was to find ways to work better together, but somehow we got offtrack. What can we do to get back to that goal?"
- "I'm not sure what happened, but this conversation has taken a turn for the worse. Can we agree to talk about what is good about the work so that can refocus the conversation on things that are more positive?"
- "Let me apologize in advance for my part in the misunderstanding. This is not the conversation that I hoped to have. Can we start over?"
- "This is not what I intended for the conversation, what about you?"
- "When we started, I was hopeful to have a good and professional conversation about work, not a heated exchange. Can we change course?"
- "This is a difficult conversation for me. Can we pause for a second while I collect myself?"
- "I can imagine that this conversation is not easy for you as it is difficult for me as well. What can we do to get back on a firm footing?"

These examples can be adopted or adapted to your work environment, normal word choice, and style of talking.

Another survival technique for when the conversation is not going as smoothly as you would like is to pass the baton to the employee and let him or her take the lead for a while. Simply asking "What questions do you have today?" or "What is on your mind?" is a good way of temporarily shifting the focus and allowing yourself to regroup. This can even be done when the conversation is going well as it ensures the employee is engaged in the conversation.

For the Record: A Meeting Summary

A brief, one-page or less summary of each performance conversation meeting can be kept. The same structured instrument potentially used to prepare for and conduct the conversation can also be used to summarize the meeting. Additional notes can be handwritten on the back of the paper. There is no need to do more or make this an onerous exercise. If one does not have an instrument, a simple, bulleted list of the major discussion points can be kept on a sheet of paper, either handwritten during the meeting or typed afterwards. A summary e-mail works great for this purpose, as well.

Both parties can keep a copy of the summary. It can be used as a reminder for each party of any agreements or conclusions formed during the meeting, a reference point if there are follow-up items from the meeting that must be addressed, or a written record. This summary can also be useful for an end-of-year discussion, if desired. A Performance Questions list like Appendix H or a Performance Conversations Checklist instrument like Appendix N can also serve as documentation of the meeting. Nothing more is needed.

The Magic Is in the Method, Not the Words
How to Hold a Thirty-Minute Conversation: A Review

Let's talk! The secret to successful relationships and partnerships is open and honest communication. The magic of the Performance Conversations methodology stems from a rich dialogue between an employee and manager that focuses on the most important aspects of work. That's it! If both have periodic, thirty-minute conversations spread over a year regarding the most pressing challenges they face at work, success will follow. The forms, processes, guides, and everything else designed for the method are meant to facilitate communication, collaboration, and coordination. Two people partnering together to produce the best possible outcomes is what the whole system is about.

The best part of the process is that it is simple, easy to do, and you can start today. You do not need the approval of upper management, the help of Human Resources, or the advice of the best consultants. Each individual manager can employ the techniques outlined here in their own area, right now. If upper management insists on using the blunt instrument known as performance appraisals and that you comply with the mandate to complete their poorly-designed form in December to justify wage increases—play along with them or risk being hit with their blunt instrument. However, remember that their purposes and yours are different. You are trying to improve performance while they are trying to fit it into a box on a form.

However, a little planning and preparation must occur before one employs the Performance Conversations method. To do so, follow these five steps:

1. Think about the three to five most important jobs of one's staff members at work.
2. Write these ideas down alongside the variables that make the most difference in determining if these actions are performed poorly or well.
3. Determine a series of questions to ask regarding the highest priorities. Questions that help determine the quality or quantity of work performed are especially important.
4. Refine and standardize these questions. Develop an instrument or simply tell staff via e-mail that these are the questions they will be asked in the future when meeting on a regular basis.
5. Schedule a series of conversations with your staff throughout the year at intervals that makes sense for your work. Determine a time period during which an employee's answers will still be relevant because their responses should be used as a basis for future decisions or actions. Send a simple e-mail saying "Come prepared to answer these questions when we meet next Friday. Bring examples, evidence, or other materials to support your answers where possible and appropriate. I look forward to our conversation."

Now, you are ready to start talking. A performance improvement system designed and implemented in less than thirty minutes by an expert—you. No one else knows the most important factors surrounding your work better.

So, just go and do it! Hold the conversation, ask a few questions, and talk—that's it. You will be surprised by what happens.

Initial Reactions and Awkward Conversations

The first conversation will be the most difficult, as you and your staff members are bound to feel varying degrees of awkwardness or skepticism. Employees will likely ask themselves questions like, "Does she really want to know my opinion and what I think and feel?" "Do you really want to know the truth?" "Will you use the truth against me or use it to help me?" "Can I really ask you for help?" "Is this real?" "Will we do this again?" "Can I ask any question that I want about work?" "Why haven't we done this before?"

The employee will fully engage if they notice how you are genuinely interested in focusing on and improving the work and their performance. However, they will disengage if they perceive that you do not care about the conversation, will use the information against them to determine a performance rating or raise, or you do not appreciate their opinions or their work. Holding an effective performance conversation is an art, and how to acquire this talent is embedded in these pages. Start with an open mind and heart and simply ask a few questions, that's all. Practice and repetition will take care of the rest.

Can We Create Some Magic Together?

Magic happens when two people work cooperatively toward a common goal. The Performance Conversations method provides a structured process that encourages the communication and collaboration necessary to producing breakthrough results. Asking questions jumpstarts the process by encouraging an open exchange of information. Two heads are better than one, and there is a multiplicative effect, a chemical reaction, an unleashing of potential that happens when people collaborate. When two people with good intentions work together, who knows what can happen?

A Final Question

The important thing is not to stop questioning.
Curiosity has its own reason for existing.

—Albert Einstein

Any intelligent fool can make things bigger, more
complex, and more violent. It takes a touch of genius—
and a lot of courage to move in the opposite direction.

—E. F. Schumacher

The Performance Conversations method proves to be an invaluable tool for performance improvement, productivity, and positive individual and organizational outcomes. It is built upon the universal idea that questions can be used to stimulate effective communication, critical thinking, analysis, problem-solving, ideation, innovation, productivity, performance improvement, and many other purposes beneficial to the workplace. The method provides a framework for holding performance conversations that reinforce the things going well, correct those not going well, and share information that can produce future successes or forestall future problems. This framework is flexible, utilitarian, and easy to employ.

Some may critique the use of questions and some may wonder why managers everywhere are not using something so simple and obvious already. The truth is good managers and experts in every field have already mastered the art of asking questions. However, this art has not been applied in a systematic way in the area of performance improvement. The Performance Conversations method remedies this oversight.

Questions Are Powerful!

Questions have power, questions are magical, and questions have the hidden capacity to stir men and women's souls by provoking new thoughts, feelings, ideas, and actions. The right question can communicate, challenge, solve, excite, compel, and cause many, many different types of reactions. This power can be harnessed to produce better performance outcomes. Questions are used in many professions and should be considered a basic management skill. Doctors use them to diagnose illnesses, lawyers use them to establish facts, therapists use them to heal, scientists use them to discover, and supervisors use them to hire—so why should managers not use them to manage performance?

Questions are natural tools for managing because they allow one to start a conversation and keep it going. In the book *Crucial Conversations*, the authors discuss a "pool of shared meaning," where we both know and exchange certain essential pieces of information. Questions are the best method of sharing and understanding what others think and know. They encourage dialogue, critical thinking, and analysis which lead to a shared understanding, shared goals, cooperation, and partnership. All challenges in the human endeavor are solved through good, healthy, open, and honest communication, whether they be marital problems, legal issues, international diplomacy, collective bargaining, or simple disagreements among friends.

Dialogue, debate, talking, exchanging information, and questioning are all ways of communicating, and good communication is necessary to building great relationships and partnerships. Good questions can be used to improve conversations and communication and therefore encourage better performance.

Can Something So Simple Really Work?

> *...the height of sophistication is simplicity.*
> —Clare Boothe Luce

As noted earlier, traditional appraisal systems have dozens of purposes; however, not many of them are oriented toward performance improvement. We have dismantled the traditional theories and presented a simple and elegant framework for meeting the complex, challenging, changing, and demanding requirements of business—asking questions. This is made more straightforward by a method and three techniques effective at eliciting the type of responses necessary to producing and reproducing better performance. There are traditionally dozens of performance management theories and approaches which require us to spend countless hours participating in a process that we know intuitively is ineffective and counterproductive. A complete dissertation on why traditional appraisals do not work is beyond the scope of this book. However, the fifteen fallacies of appraisals are detailed in *Performance Conversations: An Alternative to Appraisals* along with a more complete explanation of the Performance Conversations method foundational to the Performance Portfolio, Performance Questions, and Performance Conversations Checklists techniques.

A Simple Solution

> *Organizations that apply these simple concepts and*
> *develop the skills and discipline to ask better questions*
> *and define their problems with more rigor can create*
> *a strategic advantage, unlock truly groundbreaking*
> *innovation, and drive better business performance.*
> *Asking better questions delivers better results.*
>
> —Dwayne Spradlin[47]

Here we present a refreshingly simple, yet powerful alternative for increasing the productivity of staff—the Performance Conversations method. Peter Drucker is famous for saying "What's measured improves." Dr. John Izzo, a bestselling author and management guru, says it better: "That which is focused upon improves." The point is that when we center our attention, effort, and energy in a specific direction, good things can happen. This is the purpose of the performance improvement system outlined in this book. It is designed to start an ongoing conversation and call our attention and best efforts toward the most important aspects of our work. When we consider, discuss, and act on our highest priorities, they improve. This book provides a structured approach to achieving this end.

Come On, Ask Me a Question!

While many questions presented in this text were expertly designed to promote the best intent of every good performance management system, they can be tailored to fit local circumstances or address other pressing needs. Simple forethought and planning are all that is necessary to creating a slate of questions that can be used to cultivate rich conversations about the highest priorities of one's work. The information gathered can be used to make good decisions about which actions to take and improve performance. Good advice is to start with the Magnificent Seven Questions. After one becomes more familiar with the techniques, new questions can be introduced or substituted that reflect the specific nature of one's work environment. The best part of the approach is that you can start today. You do not need additional tools, equipment, software, hardware, or expensive training courses. So, go ahead and imagine one of your employees looking at you and saying, "Ask me a question!"

APPENDICES

Questions to Ask Your Manager

Before the Meeting

- "What do I need to bring to the meeting?"
- "What will be the primary topics of discussion at the meeting?"
- "Is there any particular work information that you are most concerned about?"
- "What evidence can I offer that will show how well I am doing?"
- "What examples can I produce to show the challenges that I am facing?"

During the Performance Conversation

- "What do I need to do to produce A+ work by the end of the year?"
- "What are the two or three things I need to work on most?"
- "Do you have any concerns with how I work?"
- "What are the most important elements of my job?"
- "Where do you think my strengths lie?"
- "What should I be working on?"
- "What are the highest priorities of work right now?"
- "What can I do to help others succeed?"
- "What can I do for you to help you succeed?"
- "Is there anything that I am missing?"

After the Meeting

- "What follow-up items should I complete before we meet again?"
- "Are there opportunities for me to do more?"

B

Questions for All Performance Improvement Occasions

What to Say When You Do Not Know What to Ask!

- "What excites you the most about what you have been doing lately?"
- "What would you like to talk about?"
- "What is on your mind?"
- "Our goal is to do the best work possible; what else should we be considering?"
- "Are we talking about things that will eventually lead to better performance outcomes?"
- "Are we talking about the right things?"
- "Are we talking about things that really matter?"
- "What is on your mind the most lately about work?"
- "What do you suggest we talk about today?"
- "What are the advantages and disadvantages of...?"
- "What do you think will result from...?"
- "What is the most challenging part of your job?"
- "How might we exceed expectations?"
- "How might we transform the team (or department)?"
- "In what area of your responsibilities do you have the greatest challenges?"
- "How can we be sure that all our goals are met?"
- "What evidence do we have that things are going well?"
- "What can we do to perform our work better?"
- "What are the three things that we should be tracking?"
- "Does that make a difference?"

- "What are our assumptions about what does and does not work?"
- "What are the options?"
- "What do you think?"
- "What have you read about lately that we might use to our advantage?"
- "What are some of the best practices in use today that we have yet to try?"
- "Can you share with me your thoughts regarding...?"
- "What is your reaction to...?"
- "What do you think are the most important parts to...?"
- "What are one or two ideas that will help us meet our goals?"
- "Do you need any additional resources?"
- "Can we start over?"
- "If you could change one thing about work, what would it be?"
- "What have you accomplished within the past two weeks that you are proudest of?"
- "Should we be satisfied with the current state of affairs, or are there other opportunities that we should pursue?"
- "What is stopping us from achieving all of our goals?"
- "Have you had the chance to do your very best work lately?"
- "Is there anything preventing you from performing at your best?"
- "Can you draw me a picture of what you are describing?"
- "What options are we not considering?"
- "Who else should share responsibility in this?"
- "How do you think I/others will react if...?"
- "Do you have any skills from volunteer activities or hobbies that are not being used at work?"
- "What do you want to be when you grow up?"
- "Who, what, when, where, why, and how?"
- "What if...?"
- "Really?"

Performance Questions for Different Situations

To Coach

- "What would you like to work on today?"
- "What are you doing when you feel like you are doing your best?"
- "How do you feel about…?"
- "What are you having the most difficulty with?"
- "What do you find most fulfilling?"

To Draw Out/Into Conversation

- "Can you tell me a little more about that?"
- "I'm not sure if I understand what you really mean, can you give me more detail?"
- "I think I understand what you're saying, but can you tell me again?"
- "Can you tell me what you're saying in a different way?"
- "Can you tell me again using different words so I can make sure I understand what you're saying?"
- "Would you explain what you mean by that?"
- "What did you mean by that?"
- "If you were describing this situation to your mother, what would you say?"

To Support or Encourage

- "What can I do to help you perform your very best?"
- "How can I recognize your best effort?"
- "What do you want to be when you grow up?"
- "If there were no constraints, how would you approach your work?"
- "What would make your work more fulfilling?"

To Direct or Redirect

- "Do you know what you should be doing every day?"
- "Can you tell me what you think are the three to five highest priorities of your work?"
- "Do you know what you do that makes the most difference or has the biggest impact?"
- "Can you describe how to work on _____ to make sure that it is right?"
- "If you could do things over, what would you do differently?"

To Reinforce

- "What did you do next?"
- "How do we produce this level of quality each and every time?"
- "What did you notice you did this time as compared to other times?"

To Probe or Prompt

- "What would you do if you were in my position?"
- "What are the missing ingredients to greater success?"
- "What are the 'white elephants' that people are reluctant to discuss?"

Regarding Resources (Support, Tools, and Equipment)

- "Do you have everything you need to be successful?"
- "What is preventing you from producing A+ work?"
- "What would you do differently if you had unlimited resources?"
- "What do you need to be successful?"

For Remediation

- See Appendix F: Questions for Difficult Conversations and Difficult Employees

Questions to Ask Yourself (for Managers)

- "What do I need to do to prepare for this conversation?"
- "Do I have evidence to show the work we have been doing?"
- "Where are my function/departmental goals?"
- "Have I shared all the information I can with staff about things that are important?"
- "What resources can I provide my team that they do not already have?"
- "What are the top three priorities of work right now?"
- "Have I communicated the top priorities?"
- "Have I communicated the top goals?"
- "What are the factors that affect the top priorities?"
- "How do I know what is successful?"
- "Do staff members need more training?"
- "Are staff members clear on the things for which they are accountable?"
- "Do staff understand my work as a manager and know how they help me and the department succeed?"
- "Does my staff know what to do when I am not at work or unavailable?"
- "Does my staff know what to do in emergencies?"
- "Does my staff know how to rely on and support one another?"
- "Does my supervision style help or hinder staff performance?"
- "What can I do to advance company/organizational goals?"
- "Have I recognized the right employees for their work lately?"
- "Have I said 'thank you' to the appropriate employees lately?"

- "Have I said encouraging words to the necessary employees lately?"
- "Have I rewarded the appropriate employees recently?"
- "What can I do today to encourage or support my staff's success?"
- "What are the trouble signs that things are not going well?"
- "How do we determine the right evidence to collect?"
- "What are the most important things that we should be tracking?"
- "What are the measures, metrics, and indicators of quality outcomes?"
- "What are the three most important statistics regarding our work?"
- "What does senior management need to know about what we are doing?"
- "Have I invited employees to make improvement suggestions?"
- "Which employees need my help the most and why?"
- "What are the items that only I can address?"
- "What patterns have emerged from recent conversations with...?"
- "What are the three biggest challenges we face at work?"
- "What are the recurrent successes with work and why?"

Questions to Ask in Preparation of a Performance Conversation (for Managers)

- "What evidence do we have that shows how well work is going?"
- "What evidence is missing that justifies the work we do?"
- "What evidence should we track to provide a clear picture of our work?"
- "What incidents give us the best examples of what good work looks like?"
- "What behaviors—good and bad—do we need to discuss?"
- "Is there a pattern emerging in the activities related to work (efforts, outcomes, and behaviors)?"
- "What good work do we need to repeat?"
- "What poor work activity or behavior do we need to avoid or adjust?"
- "What general information should we share that is important to discuss?"
- "What are the follow-up items from the last performance discussion?"
- "What are the quarterly or annual goals that we need to address?"
- "What are the key items for today's discussion?"
- "Are there strategic considerations that we should discuss?"
- "What are the things that I can do to assist this individual employee?"
- "What are the biggest challenges about work right now?"
- "What are the biggest challenges with (employee name) right now?"
- "What has (employee name) done well or poorly lately?"

- "How can I recognize (employee name) for their recent work?"
- "What can I say to encourage…?"
- "What personal tidbits can I discuss with my employee today to build rapport?" (e.g. The success of my child's soccer team knowing that she is a soccer fan as well, her vacation plans to a place I've also visited, etc.)

Questions for Difficult Conversations and Difficult Employees

Note: Many of these questions start with a statement of fact in order to diffuse a situation and segue into the issue at hand.

- "How do we avoid the mistakes of the past?"
- "What will you do differently when you leave this room?"
- "What happened just before you made the earlier mistake?"
- "I have some concerns and I'm curious if you do so as well. If so, what are they?"
- "Do you think that things are going well?"
- "Do you think that things are going well with your coworkers?"
- "Do you agree that getting along with others is as important as the work we do, especially considering how no one works alone in any organization?"
- "Do you agree or disagree that behavior is as important to performance as performance is itself? Why?"
- "How we work with others makes a difference; how would you respond to this idea?"
- "I do not think that things are going as well as they could be; what do you think?"
- "Are things going as well as you would like?"
- "On a scale from one to ten, where would you rate your performance and why? Use examples, please."
- "How do you think you compare to others doing similar work?"
- "How well do you think you get along with others compared to your coworkers?"

- "Do you feel good about the work that you do every day? Why?"
- "What do you believe your coworkers think about your work?"
- "How do you think others view your work and why?"
- "Many experts say that excellent performance includes what you do and how you do it. What do you think about this statement?"
- "Everybody sees things differently, so can you tell me how you see…?"
- "Understanding that we may not agree on everything, what do you think about _____? Why?"
- "Do you think the work that you do is valued?"
- "Do you feel you get the credit you deserve for your work?"
- "Assuming we will disagree about the quality of your work, can you tell me why you think we will disagree? On which points do you think we will disagree?"
- "Do you think you get too little or too much credit for the work you do? Why?"
- "What do you think I believe about your work? Why?"
- "Since things are not ideal currently, what can we do differently to make things right?"
- "Who do you think you should emulate at work?"
- "Performance can be defined as efforts, outcomes, and behaviors. What do you think about that statement?"
- "We are all responsible for our actions and failures. What does this mean to you?"
- "Some things are not connecting for me and I'm not sure why. Can you help me understand why I'm sensing things are not going well?"
- "Some things don't add up, but can you tell me what you think?"
- "What concrete evidence do you have that offers a different interpretation of the facts?"
- "Can you give me a full description of how you go about _____ from A to Z?"

Questions to Ask Myself (for Employees)

- "Am I aware of the policies and procedures that affect how my work is completed?"
- "Am I aware of the policies and procedures related to assignments, pay, promotions, and other things that affect my employment?"
- "Am I aware of and do I understand the human resources policies that affect both me and my position?"
- "What resources do I need to do my very best work?"
- "Do I have enough resources to do a good job?"
- "What do I need generally to do my very best work?"
- "Do I have the right tools and equipment?"
- "What are two actions that would improve the quality of my work if I took them today?"
- "What is stopping me from doing my very best work?"
- "What do I enjoy most about my work?"
- "What do I enjoy least about my work?"
- "What makes me dread coming to work?"
- "What makes me look forward to coming to work every day?"
- "What do I do best?"
- "What would I like to do more of?"
- "What would I like to learn?"
- "Which of my coworkers do I enjoy working with the most?"
- "Which of my coworkers do I enjoy working with the least?"
- "Out of my coworkers, who helps me perform my responsibilities the best?"
- "Which of my coworkers can I help perform better?"

- "Which departments are good to work with and which are a chore?"
- "Do I know how to do everything for which I am responsible?"
- "Do I know the best way to complete all of my assignments?"
- "What excuses do I have for not producing A+ work?"
- "What can I ask my manager/supervisor to do that would make my work easier/better?"
- "What ideas for improvement can I share with my manager?"

Performance Questions Instrument: Magnificent Seven (Sample)

Performance Questions

These questions are designed to be conversation starters. The goal is to ensure we discuss the most important things about work each time we meet.

General Questions

- What is going well?
- What is not going well?
- What else is going on?
- What is the status of your goals, action plans, and follow-up items?
- What can I do for you?
- How are your professional relationships going?
- How are you?

Supervisor's Signature: _____
Date: _____

In advance of the next meeting, remind the employee of the conversation and ask that they prepare, then review your supervisor's log to note the employee's contributions over the most recent discussion period. During the meeting, record your observations of the employee's performance in response to each of the questions above and then compile any evidence that supports your observations.

Performance Questions Instrument: Big 3 (Sample)

Performance Questions	
What is going well?	What is not going well?
What else is going on? (information to share)	Other
Employee _____ Date _____	Supervisor _____ Date _____

J

Performance Questions
Instrument: My Work (Sample)

Performance Questions for ACME General

General Questions
- What is going well?
- What is not going well?
- What else is going on?

Division/Team Questions
- What is the status of your annual goals, action plans, and follow-up items from our last meeting?
- What are some of the benefits you have found using our new system?
- What have been your successes and failures related to establishing new customers?
- How might we improve our business processes?

My Company Questions
- Do you know how your work is connected to the company's _____ (year) strategic goals?
- Have you completed your professional development goals for the year?

Questions specifically for _____ (employee's name): *(e.g. duties, tasks, reports, development, performance, etc.)*

Other
- How do your job description and your actual job duties differ?
- What training do you need to get you ready for promotion?
- Do you have any concerns about your position, pay, or career advancement?

Supervisor's Signature: _____

Date: _____

Performance Questions Instrument: Prep (Sample)

Performance Conversations
Preparation Instrument—Leader

_____

Employee's Name

This form is designed to be a conversation starter to keep the focus on the most important things about work. Ask employees questions about the categories of work below and record their answers.

Goals

Competencies

Business Development

Projects

Learning Goals

Supervisor's Signature: _____
Date: _____
Employee's Signature: _____
Date: _____

Performance Questions Instrument: Sales Prep (Sample)

Performance Conversations
Preparation Instrument—Leader

_____

Employee's Name

This form is designed to start a conversation and keep it focused. In advance of the next meeting, remind the employee of the conversation and ask that they prepare. They should respond to the three to five most important aspects of work, which are predefined, unchanging, and established in advance of each meeting. You and the employee should each report on what you each think are the most important things currently happening at work, then compare notes. Review your supervisor's log to ensure you have recorded these observations and compile any evidence that supports your notes, including Performance Logs, Performance Portfolios, e-mails, reports, etc.

What is going well?

Sales/Goals/Project A/Client A
Leads/Strategies/Project B/Client B
Repeat business/Objectives/Project C/Client C

What is not going well?

Sales:
Leads:
Repeat Business:

What other information should we share?

Sales:

Leads:

Repeat Business:

Other observations*: Things to focus on and discuss (e.g. reports, development, goals, competencies, etc.)*

Follow-up items*: What should have been completed since the last performance conversation by _____(employee name) and me?*

Supervisor's Signature: _____

Date: _____

Employee's Signature: _____

Date: _____

Performance Questions Instrument: Customers (Sample)

Performance Questions	
1. Can you tell me about your understanding of the company's new customer service initiative?	2. Do you know how your job contributes to delivering world-class customer service?
3. On a scale of 1–10, how would you rate your customer service effort and the efforts of your peers? Why? (Please use examples.) Employee's effort? Peer's effort? Comments:	4. Do you have any suggestions for what the company and your department can do to improve customer service?
Employee _____ Date _____	Supervisor _____ Date _____

Performance Conversations Checklist: Priorities (Sample)

Performance Discussion Checklist					
	1st Quarter	2nd Quarter	3rd Quarter	4th Quarter	Remarks
Review of priorities	☐	☐	☐	☐	
Discussion of concerns	☐	☐	☐	☐	
Needs (tools and resources)	☐	☐	☐	☐	
Goal attainment	☐	☐	☐	☐	
Celebrations	☐	☐	☐	☐	
Other	☐	☐	☐	☐	
Professional development plan		☐		☐	
Job description update				☐	
Comments:					
Employee Initials	RBL	RBL	RBL		
Supervisor Initials	MGE	MGE	MGE		
Dates	3/24/__	6/30/__	9/29/__		

Performance Conversations Checklist: Magnificent Seven (Sample)

One-On-One Conversation Checklist			
	1st Trimester	2nd Trimester	3rd Trimester
What is going well?	☐	☐	☐
What is not going well?	☐	☐	☐
What else is going on?	☐	☐	☐
What is the status of your goals and plans?	☐	☐	☐
How are your professional relationships?	☐	☐	☐
What can I do for you?	☐	☐	☐
How are you?	☐	☐	☐
Other:	☐	☐	☐
Comments:			
Employee Initials			
Supervisor Initials			
Dates:	4/30/___	8/31/___	

Performance Conversations Checklist: Sales (Sample)

Salespersons Bi-Monthly Pep Talk						
Instructions: Both the supervisor and the employee write their initials under the appropriate column to indicate when each item was discussed.						
Topics to Discuss	**FEB**	**APR**	**JUN**	**AUG**	**OCT**	**DEC**
Sales volume (challenges and successes)	—— ——	—— ——	—— ——	—— ——	—— ——	—— ——
Success with leads	—— ——	—— ——	—— ——	—— ——	—— ——	—— ——
Patronage metrics	—— ——	—— ——	—— ——	—— ——	—— ——	—— ——
Exchange ideas for improvement	—— ——	—— ——	—— ——	—— ——	—— ——	—— ——
Company strategic goals and my contributions	—— ——	—— ——	—— ——	—— ——	—— ——	—— ——
Things needed from manager	—— ——	—— ——	—— ——	—— ——	—— ——	—— ——
Follow-up items to discuss next time:						
Other:						

Performance Conversations Checklist: Needs (Sample)

All I Need To Succeed Checklist
This conversation is designed to focus on all the things one needs to be successful. If something is not listed here, please bring it up in the conversation. There should not be any obstacles to one's success. Select **yes**, **no**, or **other** for each item, providing comments as needed.

1st Quarter	Y	N	O	2nd Quarter	Y	N	O
• Do I know what to do to be successful?	☐	☐	☐	• What would I change if I could?	☐	☐	☐
• Do I know why what I do matters?	☐	☐	☐	• What would produce better outcomes?	☐	☐	☐
• Do I have all the support I need?	☐	☐	☐	• What obstacles inhibit my work?	☐	☐	☐
• Do I have enough tools and resources?	☐	☐	☐	• What do I enjoy most about work?	☐	☐	☐
• Do I have any unmet training needs?	☐	☐	☐	• Am I challenged and fulfilled? Why?	☐	☐	☐
• Other	☐	☐	☐	• Other	☐	☐	☐
Comments				**Comments**			
How do I feel about today's conversation?				How do I feel about today's conversation?			
Date _____				Date _____			
Initials _____				Initials _____			

3rd Quarter	Y	N	O	4th Quarter	Y	N	O
• Do I know what to do to be successful?	☐	☐	☐	• What would I change if I could?	☐	☐	☐
• Do I know why what I do matters?	☐	☐	☐	• What would produce better outcomes?	☐	☐	☐
• Do I have all the support I need?	☐	☐	☐	• What obstacles inhibit my work?	☐	☐	☐
• Do I have enough tools and resources?	☐	☐	☐	• What do I enjoy most about work?	☐	☐	☐
• Do I have any unmet training needs?	☐	☐	☐	• Am I challenged and fulfilled? Why?	☐	☐	☐
• Other	☐	☐	☐	• Other	☐	☐	☐
Comments				**Comments**			
How do I feel about today's conversation?				How do I feel about today's conversation?			
Date _____ Initials _____				Date _____ Initials _____			

Performance Conversations Checklist: Topics (Sample)

Quarterly Check-In Conversation			
This is an occasion to talk about the most important things going on at work. It is about what is going well, not going well, and whatever else needs to be discussed. In addition to these topics, here are other ideas that can be discussed depending upon the needs of the work environment:			

- Successes
- Concerns
- Opportunities

- KPI's
- Recognition
- Strategy Alignment

- Training/Resource needs
- Career development
- Other

	Discussion	Goals	Initials
July–September		☐ Completed ☐ On track ☐ Offtrack ☐ Not Started	_____ _____
October–December		☐ Completed ☐ On track ☐ Offtrack ☐ Not Started	_____ _____
January–March		☐ Completed ☐ On track ☐ Offtrack ☐ Not Started	_____ _____
April–June		☐ Completed ☐ On track ☐ Offtrack ☐ Not Started	_____ _____
Other:			
Employee Name:		Department:	
Supervisor Name:			

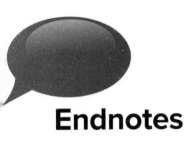

Endnotes

1. Terry J. Fadem, *The Art of Asking: Ask Better Questions, Get Better Answers* (Upper Saddle River, NJ: Pearson Education, 2009).
2. Leon Neyfakh, "Are We Asking the Right Questions?," *Boston Globe*, May 20, 2012, https://www.bostonglobe.com/ideas/2012/05/19/just-ask/k9PATXFdpL6ZmkreSiRYGP/story.html.
3. Thomas Cleary, *Zen Lessons: The Art of Leadership* (Boulder, CO: Shambhala, 2004).
4. Dan Rothstein and Luz Santana, *Make Just One Change: Teach Students to Ask Their Own Questions* (Cambridge, MA: Harvard Education Press, 2011).
5. Andrew Sobel and Jerold Panas, *Power Questions: Build Relationships, Win New Business, and Influence Others* (Hoboken, NJ: Wiley, 2012).
6. Sobel and Panas.
7. Diana Whitney and Amanda Trosten-Bloom, *The Power of Appreciative Inquiry: A Practical Guide to Positive Change*, 2nd ed. (Oakland, CA: Berrett-Koehler Publishers, 2010).
8. Patricia Burgin in discussion with the author, February 2020.
9. Peter Cappelli and Anna Tavis, "The Performance Management Revolution," *Harvard Business Review*, October 2016, 58–67.
10. Cappelli and Tavis, 58–67.
11. Amy Jen Su, "How to Give Feedback to People Who Cry, Yell or Get Defensive," *Harvard Business Review*, September 21, 2016, https://hbr.org/2016/09/how-to-give-feedback-to-people-who-cry-yell-or-get-defensive.
12. Cheyna Brower and Nate Dvorak, "Why Employees Are Fed Up With Feedback," *Gallup at Work*, October 2019, https://www.gallup.com/workplace/267251/why-employees-fed-feedback.aspx.
13. Cappelli and Tavis, 58–67.

14. Reuters, "SAP, Maker of Performance Review Software, Ditches Performance Reviews," *Fortune*, August 12, 2016, https://fortune.com/2016/08/12/sap-ends-performance-reviews/.

15. Workpop. "Millennials Are Inspiring a New Approach to Performance Reviews," *Inc.*, November 15, 2017, https://www.inc.com/workpop/how-continuous-feedback-can-transform-your-performance-reviews-for-better.html.

16. TriNet, "Survey: Performance Reviews Drive One in Four Millennials to Search for a New Job or Call in Sick," (Press Release, October 27, 2015), https://www.trinet.com/about-us/news-press/press-releases/survey-performance-reviews-drive-one-in-four-millennials-to-search-for-a-new-job-or-call-in-sick.

17. TriNet.

18. Tom Gimbel, "Why Your Younger Employees Hate Performance Reviews," *Fortune*, February 13, 2017, https://fortune.com/2017/02/13/millennial-employees-performance-reviews/.

19. Deloitte, "The Deloitte Global Millennial Survey 2019," https://www2.deloitte.com/global/en/pages/about-deloitte/articles/millennialsurvey.html.

20. Stuart Hearn, "6 Things Millennials Want From the Performance Management Process," *Training Magazine*, January 24, 2017, https://trainingmag.com/6-things-millennials-want-performance-management-process/.

21. "To Feed Forward or to Feedback? That is the Question," Metasysteme, accessed January 24, 2020, https://www.metasysteme-coaching.eu/english/to-feed-back-or-to-feed-forward/.

22. Kevin Kruse, "Stop Giving Feedback, Instead Give Feedforward," *Forbes*, July 19, 2012, https://www.forbes.com/sites/kevinkruse/2012/07/19/feedforward-coaching-for-performance/#2922263a235d.

23. David Cooperrider, "Mirror Flourishing and the Design of Positive Institutions," *David Cooperridge* (blog), September 2, 2015, https://www.davidcooperrider.com/2015/09/02/mirror-flourishing-and-the-design-of-positive-institutions/.

24. Gervase R. Bushe and Aniq F. Kassam, "When Is Appreciative Inquiry Transformational? A Meta-Case Analysis," *Journal of Applied Behavioral Science*, 41 (2005): 161–181. Jacqueline Bascobert Kelm, *Appreciative living: The principles of appreciative inquiry in personal life* (Wake Forest, NC: Venet, 2005).

25. Avraham N. Kluger and Dina Nir, "The Feedforward Interview," *Human Resource Management Review* 20, no. 3 (2010): 235-246, https://doi.org/10.1016/j.hrmr.2009.08.002.

26. Kluger and Nir, 235–246.

27. Kluger and Nir, 235-246.

28. Marie-Helene Budworth, Gary P. Latham, and Laxmikant Manroop, "Looking Forward to Performance Improvement: A Field Test of the Feedforward Interview for Performance Management," *Human Resource Management* 54, no. 1 (2015): 45-54, https://doi.org/10.1002/hrm.21618.

29. Bridget Rice, "Feedforward or Feedback—Reframing Positive Performance Management," *Human Resource Management International Digest* 25, no. 5 (2017): 7-9, https://doi.org/10.1108/HRMID-04-2017-0060. Kluger and Nir, 235-246. Osnat Bouskila-Yam and Avraham N. Kluger, "Strength-based performance appraisal and goal setting," *Human Resource Management Review*, 21, (2011): 137–147.

30. Annamarie Mann and Ryan Darby, "Should Managers Focus on Performance or Engagement?" *Gallup Business Journal*, August 5, 2014, https://news.gallup.com/businessjournal/174197/managers-focus-performance-engagement.aspx.

31. David Horsager, "The 2019 Trust Outlook," *Trust Edge Leadership Institute* (2019) http://trustedge.com/wp-content/uploads/2018/10/2019-Trust-Outlook.pdf.

32. Fadem.

33. Bernard T. Ferrari, *Power Listening: Mastering the Most Critical Business Skill of All* (Kennett Square, PA: Soundview Executive Book Summaries, 2012).

34. Tony Stoltzfus, "Asking Profound Questions: Five Reasons," *Coach22* (blog), January 17, 2011, https://www.coach22.com/asking-profound-questions/.

35. Marilee Adams, "Good Question?," *Empower Magazine*, February-March 2009, 4.

36. Stoltzfus, "Asking Profound Questions."

37. Atul Gawande, *The Checklist Manifesto: How to Get Things Right* (New York: Picador Paper, 2011).

38. Gawande.

39. Gawande.

40. Matthew Johnston, "Airplane Preflight," *Calaero* (blog), May 24, 2018, https://calaero.edu/airplane-preflight-checklist/.

41. Gawande.

42. Gawande.

43. Sobel and Panas.

44. Fadem.

45. Fadem.

46. Tony Stoltzfus, *Coaching Questions: A Coach's Guide to Powerful Asking Skills* (Virginia Beach, VA: Coach22, 2008).

47. Dwayne Spradlin, "Are You Solving the Right Problem? Most Firms Aren't, and That Undermines Their Innovation Efforts," *Harvard Business Review*, September 2012, 85-93.

References

Dunlap, Cheryl. "Effective Evaluation through Appreciative Inquiry." *Performance Improvement* 47, no. 2 (2008): 23-29. https://onlinelibrary.wiley.com/doi/abs/10.1002/pfi.181.

Gilbert, Jay. "The Millennials: A New Generation of Employees, a New Set of Engagement Policies." *Ivey Business Journal* (2011). https://iveybusinessjournal.com/publication/the-millennials-a-new-generation-of-employees-a-new-set-of-engagement-policies/.

Goldberg, Marilee, C. *The Art of the Question: A Guide to Short-Term Question-Centered Therapy.* New York: Wiley, 1997.

Hearn, Stuart. "Using 'Feedforward' in Employee Performance Reviews." *Clear Review* (blog). June 3, 2015. https://www.clearreview.com/feedforward-employee-performance-reviews/.

Horsager, David. *The Trust Edge: How Top Leaders Gain Faster Results, Deeper Relationships, and a Stronger Bottom Line.* New York: Free Press, 2009.

Lee, Christopher D. *Performance Conversations: An Alternative to Appraisal.* Tucson, AZ: Fenestra, 2006.

McKinney, Phil. *Beyond the Obvious: Killer Questions That Spark Game-Changing Innovation.* New York: Hyperion, 2011.

Miller, John G. *QBQ: The Question Behind the Question: Practicing Personal Accountability at Work and in Life.* Denver: Denver Press, 2001.

Miller, Stephen. "Ratingless Reviews and Pay Practices." *SHRM Online*, June 17, 2016. https://www.shrm.org/resourcesandtools/hr-topics/compensation/pages/ratingless-reviews-positively-affect-pay-practices.aspx.

Robbins, Stever. "How Leaders Use Questions." *Harvard Business School Working Knowledge*, January 19, 2004. https://hbswk.hbs.edu/archive/how-leaders-use-questions.

Samuels, Neil. "An Appreciative Performance Appraisal Conversation." *AI Commons.* Accessed January 24, 2020. https://appreciativeinquiry. champlain.edu/educational-material/an-appreciative-performance-appraisal-conversation/.

Schwantes, Marcel. "Research Confirms What We All Suspected. Millennials in the Workplace Are Not That Different from Other Generations." *Inc.,* May 30, 2018. http://www.inc.com/marcel-schwantes/research-confirms-what-we-all-suspected-millennials-in-workplace-are-not-that-different-from-other-generations.html.

Seligman, Martin E. P. *Flourish: A Visionary New Understanding of Happiness and Well-Being.* New York: Atria Books, 2011.

Stewart, Jeanine S., Elizabeth Goad Oliver, Karen S. Cravens, and Shigehiro Oishi. "Managing Millennials: Embracing Generational Differences." *Business Horizons* 60, no. 1 (2017): 45–54. https://doi.org/10.1016/j.bushor.2016.08.011.

Watts, Duncan J. *Everything is Obvious Once You Know the Answer: How Common Sense Fails Us.* New York: Crown Business, 2011.

Wright, Aliah D. "Tech Company SAP Eliminates Annual Performance Reviews." *SHRM Online,* August 18, 2016. https://www.shrm.org/resourcesandtools/hr-topics/technology/pages/sap-eliminates-annual-performance-reviews.aspx.

Index

About the Author

Christopher D. Lee, Ph.D., SHRM-SCP, SPHR, is a human resources practitioner, lecturer, researcher, and author. His background includes serving as the chief human resources officer for various colleges and universities, including Bates College and the Virginia Community College System. He is currently the chief human resources officer for William & Mary and teaches graduate human resources courses as an adjunct professor at the University of Richmond.

He is a former question writer for one of the HR profession's certification examinations and his chosen areas of expertise are recruitment, selection, performance management, and HR strategy. Chris is the author of numerous HR articles and four books, including *Performance Conversations: An Alternative to Appraisals* and *Search Committees: A Comprehensive Guide to Successful Faculty, Staff, and Administrative Searches.* He is currently completing a series of management fables based upon the adventures of a typical HR superstar manager.

His Performance Conversations method has been adopted by many companies and organizations, large and small, to include a $7 billion subsidiary of a *Fortune* 500 company and top-tier colleges and universities in the United States, Canada, Australia, and South Africa. Chris is a sought-after consultant and keynote speaker on alternative performance management systems and other HR topics. He is a graduate of Auburn, Golden Gate, and Georgia State Universities having earned a master's degree in HR Management, and a Doctor of Philosophy degree in HR Development. He is twice certified as a senior human resources professional and he is a retired Lieutenant Colonel from the United States Marine Corps Reserves. For more information about the Performance Conversations method, contact him at chris@performanceconversations.com, or www.performanceconversations.com.